THE WANDERINGS
OF ODYSSEUS
The Story of THE ODYSSEY

For Virginia - A.L.

ROSEMARY SUTCLIFF

THE WANDERINGS OF ODYSSEUS

The Story of THE ODYSSEY

Illustrated by ALAN LEE

FRANCES LINCOLN

The Wanderings of Odysseus copyright © Frances Lincoln Limited 1995
Text copyright © Anthony Lawton 1995
Illustrations copyright © Alan Lee 1995

First published in Great Britain in 1995 by
Frances Lincoln Limited, 2-4 Torriano Mews
Torriano Avenue, London NW5 2RZ

British Library Cataloguing in Publication Data
available on request

ISBN 0-7112-0862-X

Set in Bembo roman by Goodfellow and Egan Ltd, Cambridge

Printed and bound in Great Britain

1 3 5 7 9 8 6 4 2

CONTENTS

PROLOGUE

THE STORY OF the siege of Troy I have already told in another book. That was the story of how golden Helen left her husband Menelaus, the King of Sparta, to go with Prince Paris to his home in Troy; and how the black ships gathered from all the kingdoms and the islands of Greece at the summons of Agamemnon the High King, and sailed to conquer the city and bring Helen back.

The siege lasted for nine years, and many great heroes both Greek and Trojan died in the fighting before all was done. But at last, by a cunning device of Odysseus, King of Ithaca (not for nothing did men call him Odysseus the Resourceful), a Greek war-band was smuggled inside the city, hidden in the hollow belly of a huge wooden horse. And in the dark of night they opened the city gates and let their comrades in.

So Troy was taken and sacked. The warriors were slain, and their women carried off as slaves, all save Helen, whose husband brought her on board his ship with all honour to be his queen once more.

And the black ships sailed for home.

Once at sea the great fleet divided, each leader taking his own ships and setting a course for his own landing shore. And some of them came safe home, and some of them met with disaster by the way; and some, like Agamemnon, came safe home but found disaster waiting for them when they got there.

This is the story of Odysseus, and the many adventures he met with on the long sea-road back to Ithaca.

THE SACKER OF CITIES

ALMOST AS SOON AS Odysseus had parted his twelve ships from the main fleet, the south-east wind took them and carried them to the coast of Thrace, close to where the town of Ismarus was set between the mountains and the sea.

Now the Thracians had been allies of Troy during the war, and Odysseus' men considered themselves still at war with them. So they landed, and took and plundered the town, all save the house of Maron, priest of Apollo, amid its sacred laurel grove. Maron and his wife and child, Odysseus took under his protection, ordering his men back from the sacred place. And the priest was grateful. He was rich, and he made Odysseus splendid gifts at their parting: much gold, and a silver mixing bowl, and twelve huge clay jars of wine, rich and dark and so strong that in the mixing bowl it needed only one measure of wine to twenty of water.

Odysseus' men, when they had finished the plundering and carried their spoils back to the ships, would not set sail that evening but, seeing that they had good wine of their own taking and there were fat cattle to be had close by, sat eating and drinking on the shore all night long. And while they feasted, men from the town slipped out and ran to warn the people in the farms and outlying settlements; and the men they warned put on their fighting gear and took the weapons from their walls and crept down through the dark. And at dawn they attacked the Greeks on the shore.

The Greeks were woolly-witted with so much eating and drinking. They put up the stoutest fight they could; but it was a running fight back to their ships, and when they pushed off and headed for the open sea, they left more than seventy of their number lying dead along the beach.

Then another wind took them, a great storm wind that there could be no beating against. And for nine days and nights they ran before it, until on the tenth day they found refuge, and beached the ships upon the white sand that fringed a green and gentle island. The storm had sunk away, and they landed and filled their water casks at a spring that bubbled up through ferns and moss; and Odysseus sent three men to see if they could find the islanders, and make sounds of peace to them in the hope of food and help for their journey.

The three did not come back, and in a while Odysseus, growing anxious, called out two more men, each armed with a spear, and himself went with them to look for the missing three.

Now, the people of that island were kind and friendly. But they ate nothing but the fruit of the lotus flowers that grew there, and whoever tasted that fruit lost all knowledge of past and future, all wish to be up and doing, and drowsed their time away, always in the present moment of warm sunshine and dappled shade, dreaming happy dreams and forgetting all the world.

When Odysseus found his three missing seamen, they were sitting among the islanders, smiling happily with empty eyes and clearly no thought of ever going home. Then he knew what place this was, and that they had eaten of the lotus fruit.

No use to call them by name, no use to speak to them of their waiting families. "Up!" he roared at them. "Up, worthless spawn of jellyfish!" And with the help of the two who had come with him, he hauled them to their feet, and beating them with spear-shafts, drove them back to the ships.

He bound their hands and feet – there was no spark of fight in them – and flung them on board, shouting to his men to break out the sails; and again they headed for the open sea.

THE CYCLOPS

SEVEN MORE DAYS at sea brought Odysseus and his fleet to an island of rough low hills, where a deep-set bay opened toward them; there, in the mouth of the bay, they found a small and most beautiful islet that looked never to have felt the feet of any but the wild goats which grazed there. They beached their ships on the sheltered landward side, and passed the night feasting on fresh meat and the wine of Maron, priest of Apollo, thankful to rest from the sea whose waves pounded the outer side of the islet.

Next day, Odysseus took his own ship and a great jar of the priest's wine in case of need and, leaving all the rest, went to see what kind of people lived on the main island; for they could see the faint waft of distant fires, even hear faint and far off the bleating of sheep. And again, as with the Lotus Eaters, he wished to be sure whether or not the people were dangerous.

The crossing of the bay was quickly made, and Odysseus chose twelve men from his crew and pushed on inland. They had not gone far when they came upon a cave, its high entrance overhung with laurel bushes, and all about it large stone-walled folds such as men build to hold their flocks at night. Some of the folds were already filled with lambs and kids, but there was no sign of the grown flock, nor of the shepherd; so it must be that he had driven them out to pasture. Odysseus and his band prowled into the cave and looked about them. They found great baskets full of cheeses, huge pails brimming with milk and whey, but no sign or sound of life save for the bleating of the lambs from the folds outside.

The seamen wanted to take some cheeses and as many of the lambs and kids as they could carry and be off back to the ship. But Odysseus,

11

always one for seeing whatever was to be seen, wanted to get a sight of the cave's owner before they left. So they ate some of the cheese, being hungry, and settled down at the back of the cave to wait.

Towards sunset, a great bleating and pattering and all the sounds of a flock arose outside; a shadow fell across the entrance, and in came a monster shaped like a man but larger than any mortal, with only one eye, and that one round and hideous in the middle of his forehead. And at sight of him the Greeks knew that they had come to the land of Cyclopes: one-eyed sons of Poseidon, the god of the sea, who lived in caves with their sheep and did not plant or sow, for wheat and vines grew wild for them. And they knew also that they were in deadly danger.

The giant flung down a huge bundle of dry wood that he had brought in for his evening fire. Then he drove in his ewes and with them the lambs and kids, leaving the rams penned outside, and, picking up a huge flat stone, set it across the cave mouth for a door. Twenty-two yoke of horses could not have dragged away that stone. Then he set himself to milking his ewes and she-goats, carefully putting her young to each mother as he finished. The milk he set aside in pails to be drunk or made into cheese.

And all this while, the Greeks sat very still in the deep-most inner end of the cave, cold-afraid and crouching in the dark.

But the darkness could not shield them for long, for the one-eyed giant was making his evening fire and, as the flames sprang up, the red light licked into the furthest corner of the cave and found them crouching there.

"Strangers!" roared the Cyclops when he saw them, in a voice like stones grating together on a beach. "What brings you here over the highways of the sea? Traders, are you? Or pirates sucking up other men's goods and gear?"

"We are Greeks," Odysseus told him, "men from the war-host of Agamemnon, who have been long years besieging Troy. Now, with Troy fallen, we are on our way back to our own land; but winds and tides have carried our ships into strange seas; and we are come to you, hoping in the name of Zeus the All-Father that you will show us the kindness and hospitality that men show to way-weary guests beneath their roof."

But in truth he expected little kindness in that place, and little enough kindness he and his men received.

"As to this Zeus whom you call the All-Father," said the giant, "we the Cyclopes do not care an overripe fig for him, or for all his fellow gods save for Poseidon, who is our father, for we are stronger than they are, and have no need to obey any will but our own!" And he laughed deep in his throat, and seizing two of the crouching seamen, dashed out their brains on the ground. While their comrades watched in frozen horror, he tore them limb from limb and devoured them as a mountain lion devours his kill, washing down the flesh with long drafts of milk. Then he lay down to sleep amid the huddled warmth of his flock.

As soon as he was asleep, Odysseus drew his sword and, creeping close, felt for the place under the ribs where a sword thrust would pierce the giant's liver and let out his life. But even as he did so he remembered that with the Cyclops dead, there would be no getting out of that cave for himself or his men; not with that huge stone wedged across the entrance. And he sheathed his sword and went back and sat down among them once more, only shaking his head at their questioning looks.

Morning came, and the giant ate two more men. Then he milked and drove out his ewes, returning their young to the folds; and set the great stone back in the entrance as lightly as a man replacing the lid on a quiver full of arrows, and departed, driving his flock away to their day's grazing in the hill pastures.

The Greeks were near to despair. But there was a plan forming in Odysseus' head, by which he might save at least some of them.

The giant had left his staff in the cave: a tall trunk of olive wood still green, that looked to the captive Greeks more like the mast of a ship; and from this, with the tools that he found ready to hand, Odysseus managed to hack a piece about the length of an outstretched man. He set his men to smooth and shape it as though for a spear-shaft, while he built up the fire and got it blazing again. Then he took the olive-wood pole, and sharpened one end, and plunged it into the red heart of the fire to harden, pulling it out at the right moment and hiding it under the piled sheep's dung against the cave wall.

Back came the giant at sunset, and all happened again as the night before, save that this time, scenting danger in the air and thinking that they would be safer in the cave, he brought in his whole flock, rams and all. And well it was for the Greeks that he did so.

Odysseus and his band had brought a jar of Maron's wine with them when they came exploring; and during the day Odysseus had filled one of the Cyclops' ivy-wood bowls with it, adding no drop of water to the rich and heady drink. And when the giant had eaten his hideous evening meal, Odysseus took it to him humbly as a slave, saying, "This will be better than milk for washing down human flesh."

The giant drank, and smacked his lips over the goodness of it, and demanded another bowlful. Three times he drank and demanded more, and he grew very merry and swore that for such fine drink he would make the stranger a gift. "But first," he hiccuped, "you must tell me your name, that I may feel even more friendly towards you."

"My name is Nobody," said Odysseus, who knew this kind of game.

The giant let out a bellow of laughter, "Then I shall eat the rest of your company first, and Nobody last of all, and that shall be my gift to you." And laughing still, he toppled over backwards in wine-cup sleep, with his hair almost in the fringes of the fire.

Then Odysseus brought the sharpened stake from its hiding-place and made the point hot in the fire, while the rest of his band – there were but six of them now – stood round ready and waiting. And when the point glowed clear red, they took it up and with all their strength drove it into the giant's one eye and rammed it home, and Odysseus twirled it as though it were some mighty timber drill. The huge eyeball hissed, like hot iron when men plunge it into cold water to temper it, and the giant struggled to his knees and then to his feet with a frightful shriek, tearing the still-glowing stake from his blood-streaming eye socket, and howling for help to his fellow Cyclopes who lived in caves nearby.

The giants came running, but checked outside the great entrance stone, calling back, "Who is harming you, Polyphemus, that you wake us from our sleep with this uproar?"

And the giant Polyphemus roared back, "Nobody is harming me! Nobody is killing me by his cunning!"

"Then if nobody is harming you, you have no need of anyone to help you," shouted one of the giants. "If you are sick, pray to our father Poseidon, and maybe he will give you aid." Their grumbling voices grew fainter as they all headed back to their own sleeping places. And the silent laughter stirred in Odysseus.

Wailing in agony, the blinded giant fumbled his way to the cave entrance and heaved the stone aside to get the night coolness on his wound; but he sat down in the opening, stretching out his arms on either side so that if any of his captives tried to get out, he could feel and catch them.

But Odysseus had a plan for that too. Working silently in the innermost part of the cave, he chose out the largest of the rams. And with long supple withies drawn from the giant's sleeping-place he bound them together in threes, with one of his men bound beneath the middle ram of each three, so that if the blind giant touched them he would feel only the outside rams. And the biggest and strongest ram of all he seized for himself, and clung to its underside by twisting his hands and feet in its thick belly-fleece.

By the time Odysseus had finished, it was the edge of dawn, and the sheep and goats were moving towards the cave entrance where Polyphemus sat with his arms outstretched. He felt each of them as they jostled past, but could not know of the men hidden under the bellies of his finest beasts.

The finest of all, burdened with Odysseus clinging under its belly, came last, and the giant fondled it, asking it sadly, "Dear ram, you who are so proud and beautiful and come always first among your fellows, why do you now come last of all? Is it that you are slow with sorrow for your master, whom Nobody has blinded so that he cannot see your beauty any more?"

But all of them were through at last. And out on the open turf beyond the folds, Odysseus cut free his men; and they drove the sheep down toward the ship waiting on the tide-line, Polyphemus shouting and stumbling far behind them as they went.

The crew rejoiced at their coming, then wept for the death of six of their comrades. But there was no time for grieving, and Odysseus bade them load the sheep on board and push off for the islet where they had left the other ships. Then, seeing Polyphemus stumbling along the ragged clifftop, he cupped his hands about his mouth and bleated at him in mockery. That was not wise, for the sound gave their position away, and in fury the blind giant broke off the peak of a rocky hill and flung it after them. The rock fell just ahead of the ship and raised a wave that flung her back toward the shore; Odysseus punted her off again with a stout pole, and his men bent to the oars, sending her leaping forward for open water. But Odysseus was still a little crazed with all that he had been through, and he shouted back, "If anyone asks who blinded you, tell them it was Odysseus, son of Laertes and Lord of Ithaca, Odysseus the Sacker of Cities!"

And Polyphemus flung up his arms and prayed in fury and agony to the Lord Poseidon, "Hear me, blue-haired Poseidon. If I am your son indeed, then grant me that Odysseus, Sacker of Cities, if ever he comes again to his home, comes late and alone. And when he lands from a stranger's ship, let him find black trouble waiting for him!"

And he heaved up another boulder, greater than the first, and hurled it in the direction of Odysseus' laughter. But this time it fell short and the wave that it made drove the ship forward on her way toward the islet where the rest of the fleet waited for them.

THE LORD OF THE WINDS

THEIR NEXT LANDFALL was the island of Aeolus, Lord of the Winds. Here, in a splendid palace walled with bronze and set above towering cliffs, Aeolus lived most happily with his six strong sons and six fair daughters, whom he had married to each other after the manner of the kings and queens of Egypt.

Aeolus received Odysseus and his company with great kindness and sheltered them beneath his roof for a full month, while Odysseus told him the story of the siege of Troy and his own homeward voyage so far. And when the time came for them to continue on their way, Aeolus gave them fresh supplies for the voyage. To Odysseus himself he gave a bag made from a single oxhide in which he had tied up all the winds of the world save one, a gentle west wind to carry them safe home. The bag was made fast with silver cords and stowed beneath the rowing benches of Odysseus' ship; and Aeolus bade them on no account to open it until they were safely tied up in their home harbour.

They sailed for nine days and nights never needing to touch the oars, with the west wind sweetly curving their sails; and during all that time Odysseus held his place at the steering-oar and would not trust it to anyone else. But on the tenth day they sighted Ithaca. Then Odysseus, worn out, and knowing by the familiar shape of his home hills lifting over the skyline that they were near the end of their seafaring, fell asleep. And while he slept, his crew, who all along had been filled with curiosity as to what was in the oxhide bag, began to talk among themselves.

"What is this treasure from King Aeolus that our captain keeps so closely hidden, and that must not be taken out and looked at until we come to our own landing-beach?" they said. And, "Surely the bag must be full of gold and silver, that he keeps such close guard over it; and it is only right that we should have our share in it, for we have travelled as far and suffered as much as he has!" And, "Now we are so nearly home, it can do no harm to look – just to look." For by that time they were so close to the shore that they could make out people lighting fires among the rocks.

Then they hauled the bulging bag out from under the rowing benches, and untied the silver cords.

With a whistle and a roar and a shriek the prisoned winds, the winds of the world, swooped out through the neck of the oxhide. They swirled together, filling all the space between sea and sky, and leapt upon the twelve ships, scattering them and driving them back from their home shore into unknown seas.

Odysseus, waking to the despairing cries of his crew and the turmoil all about him, knew what had happened, and in his despair came close to leaping overboard into the storm-lashed sea and making an end of himself and his wanderings then and there. But he still had his men to think of, though the evil was of their making, and he strengthened his heart within him and took command of his ship and the little tempest-driven fleet once more.

And after days and nights that they lost all count of in the chaos of wind and water, they came once more to the island of Aeolus.

But this time the Lord of the Winds had no welcome for them.

"It is clear enough that the gods must hate you!" he cried out upon them. "And my house-room and my help are not for those who are hated by the gods! Away with you, and come no more over the sea-ways to my shore!"

And he drove them away. This time there was no wind at all to swell their sails, so that they must row every cable's length of the way. And they found no land to put in to at dusk, so that they must take turns at the oars and row by night as well as by day.

But on the seventh day they sighted land, and heading towards it, they found a bay which made a safe haven with tall rocks at either side of the entrance. Odysseus bade the other ships of his fleet enter the harbour and anchor in its sheltered waters. But his own ship, whose crew had let out the winds, he would not suffer to enter, being still bitter with them. Instead, he bade them tie up to one of the rock columns at the harbour-mouth. Yet because he was their captain, he remained outside with them himself.

And well it was for him that he did so.

The nights were so short in that place that the last rays of sunset had scarcely faded in the west before the eastern sky was paling toward dawn. And before the sun was up, Odysseus sent three of his own crew ashore from the rocky headland of the harbour mouth to spy out the country.

After a while they saw a town in the distance, but before they reached it they came to a well overshadowed by trees, where a long-armed, broad-shouldered girl was drawing water. They asked her who was the king of the island, and where they might find him.

"That is my father you're wanting," she said, and laughed, as though at a private jest. "Come with me and I'll bring you to him soon enough." And she led them into the town, to a great sprawling palace in the midst of it.

But the welcome the king bestowed upon them was not so different from the welcome they had received from Polyphemus. For he no sooner saw the men than he caught up one of them and dashed his brains out against a pillar, shouting that he would have fresh meat for supper. And the other two only just contrived to escape his clutches and make a desperate run for it back to the ship.

Meanwhile, the monster-king was bellowing for his henchmen; and they came running – huge fellows more like giants than men – and gathering along the cliff-tops, they began hurling down rocks upon the ships in the little enclosed harbour beneath.

The two who had escaped from the king's hall came plunging down the headland rocks and half-sprang, half-fell into the galley tied up there beyond the harbour-mouth. And Odysseus, seeing them come, saw also what was happening to the rest of the fleet. He heard the shrieks and groans of his dying men and the splintering of ships' timbers; and he knew that there was nothing he could do for them. He drew his sword and slashed through the hawser that tied his own ship to the tall rock, shouting to his crew as he did so, "Row! In the names of all the gods, row, if you would save your hides!"

Then the rowers, with the fear of a hideous death upon them, struck the water as one man, sending the ship forward like a hound slipped from the leash, and so gained the open sea, leaving that terrible place behind them. And thankful they were for their own escape, but weeping as they rowed, for the death of so many comrades.

And Odysseus knew that blue-haired Poseidon had harkened to the prayer of the blinded Cyclops, his son. For now, out of twelve ships and their valiant crews, he had but one.

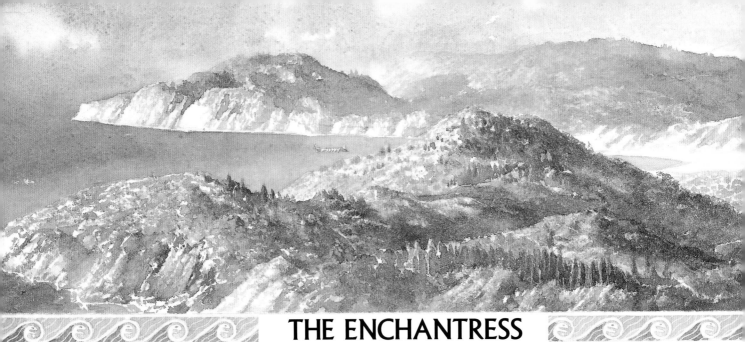

THE ENCHANTRESS

O N SAILED ODYSSEUS and the survivors of his band, until they came upon another island. Again they brought their ship into a sheltered bay; and for two days and nights they lay on a beach close beside the galley, too spent and weary to do anything more.

But when the third morning came, Odysseus took his sword and spear, and leaving the rest, struck inland in search of a vantage point from which he might see the lie of the land. Soon he came to a hill, and climbing to its crest, found himself looking out over the forest that clothed most of the island like a dark fleece, to the sea that washed its shores on every side. No sign of farmed land, no roof of any dwelling-place that he could see. But from the very heart of the island, where the trees crowded most densely together, rose a single thread of reddish smoke.

He was on the edge of pushing on to discover the meaning of that smoke, but he bethought him of the dangers of the other islands. Better maybe to return to the ship, get his men fed, and then send out a strong scouting party.

So he turned back the way he had come. And on the bank of a stream he came upon a red deer drinking under the shade of low-hanging branches. That took care of the problem of feeding his men, at all events. He speared the stag even as it took fright and leapt away; and binding its feet together with a rope of twisted withies, slung the carcass round his neck and, using his spear as a staff, set off again for the ship.

When he reached it, he found his men sitting and lying round about it, still too exhausted to care what became of them; and he flung the deer down into their midst, saying, "Hearts up! Our death day is not yet; and while there's food and drink to be had, let's feast, instead of dying of starvation!"

So they made a fire and supped that night on roast venison, and lay down to sleep with lightened hearts and full bellies.

Next morning, Odysseus divided his men into two companies and, taking command of one himself, gave the other to Eurylochus, a distant kinsman of his. And they scratched their marks on two slips of wood and put them into a helmet, shaking them up to decide which of them should go to find out the meaning of the distant feather of smoke. Eurylochus' slip leapt out, and so he set off with his two-and-twenty men into the forest, leaving Odysseus and the rest to wait with the ship.

At the day's end Eurylochus returned. He was alone, shaking and weeping, and at first he could not speak, for horror of what he had seen. But at last he grew calmer and managed to tell them what had happened.

They had come to a beautiful stone-built house at the dark heart of the forest. Tame wolves and lions were loose all around it, which came and fawned on them like hounds, or reared up to set their paws on their shoulders and lick their faces. And within the pillared foreporch they glimpsed a woman moving to and fro before her loom, and heard her voice, for she was singing softly and sweetly as she wove the delicate web.

One of the men called out to her, and she left her weaving and came out, tall and beautiful in a dark-coloured robe, with fantastic gold work on her arms and in her hair. She opened the house doors and bade them enter, and all of them save Eurylochus gladly entered at her call. But Eurylochus suspected a trap, and hid himself outside, watching through the open doors.

He saw the woman and her maidens settle his men on benches and chairs, and mix wine for them, and most sweetly and welcomingly hold the cups for them to drink.

But when they had drunk, the woman took up a slender wand of carved wood, and touched each of them in turn. And each, as she touched him, sprouted bristles and a snout and dropped on to all fours. They were no longer men but pigs, rooting and grunting all about her.

"Then," said Eurylochus, coming to the end of his tale, "she laughed and drove them out. Close by my hiding-place they passed and, following, I saw her pen them up in her pigsties, saying that was the proper place for them now. But in the filth of the sties they were weeping human tears."

When Odysseus had heard him, he slung on his sword belt, and took his bow, and bade his kinsman come back with him to the house of the enchantress. But Eurylochus crouched to his knees, weeping afresh. "I cannot – Lord, I cannot go back to that place! And do not you go there either. The men are beyond rescue, and you will never return!"

And in the end Odysseus left him with the rest, and set out through the forest alone.

But on the way he was met by Hermes, the messenger of the gods, in the likeness of a beautiful young man, who took him by the hand, saying, "Here you come through the woods alone, bent on rescuing your comrades from the pigsties of the witch Circe. But truly I think that you too will join them, but for the aid that I can give you." And he picked a plant growing at his feet and held it out, the root as black as night and the flower as white as milk. It was a plant which cannot be picked by mortal men; but to the gods all things are easy.

"Take this herb, keep it with you," said Hermes, "and the cup of enchantment which Circe will brew for you will have no power to rob you of your human shape; nor will the touch of her wand. But when she strikes you with it, you must draw your sword and leap at her as though you meant to cut her down. She will fall at your feet in terror, for no man has ever before withstood her magic, and will beg you for your goodwill and friendship; this you must grant her kindly, but not until you have made her swear to undo what she has done and work no more evil against you or your comrades."

And so saying, he was gone on his shining way back to Olympus, the home of the gods.

Odysseus thrust the plant into the breast of his tunic, where it lay cool against his skin, and went on his way. He came to the house of Circe and heard her singing at her loom, and called to her, standing in the portico with the lions and wolves fawning about him. She came out and bade him enter, and seated him in a fine chair enriched with silver and with a stool for his feet. Then she made him a posset of wine sprinkled with cheese and barley-meal and honey, and she dripped something into it from a flask she kept hidden in the hollow of her hand.

She gave the cup to Odysseus, saying, "Drink, and be welcome under my roof." And, trusting to the white-flowered plant in the breast of his tunic, he drank and set the cup down.

Then she picked up her slender wand and flicked him with it, smilingly bidding him go and join his friends in the sties outside.

But Odysseus drew his sword and made as though to run her through. With a shriek, she slipped below the blade and dropped at his feet, crying out, "Who are you, that my magic cannot touch you? Surely you must be that Odysseus who, the god Hermes once told me, would come this way in his black ship following the sea-ways home from Troy. Pray you, put up your sword, that we may learn to trust each other and be friends!"

Odysseus stood over her, still holding his sword naked in his hands. "First swear by all the gods that you will work no more evil upon me or my men. Then it may be that there can be friendship between us."

Weeping still, Circe the enchantress swore by all the gods, and Odysseus sheathed his sword.

Then her four maidens, daughters of the springs and the trees, spread fine purple rugs over the chairs, and set golden dishes on the silver tables and mixed wine in a silver bowl. They heated water and bathed Odysseus, sluicing his head and shoulders until all his weariness was washed away; and they dressed him in fine new garments and led him to the table, bidding him eat and drink.

But he sat silent, not touching the food and wine, until Circe asked him what was amiss. "Do you still doubt me?" said she. "You need have no fear. I have sworn to do you no harm."

Odysseus said, "But what of my comrades? How can I eat and be merry while they are still captive in the swine-shapes you have set upon them, and held fast in your sties?"

Then Circe went out from her hall and down to the sties, with Odysseus walking close behind her. She opened the gate and called out the swine huddled within, and touched each in turn with her wand; and as she touched them they became men again, just as they had been before, and came swiftly to their captain, flinging their arms about him and each other and weeping for joy.

29

Then the enchantress bade Odysseus go back to see his ship safely drawn up on to the beach and all their gear stowed in a nearby cave, and return with the rest of his crew, that they might all bide beneath her roof for a while.

Odysseus doubted for a moment, but his hunger after any kind of strange experience was with him still; and he knew also that he and his men needed rest and fresh supplies before they took to the sea-ways again. So he agreed, and down to the shore they all went, and told their comrades what had happened, and that Circe wished to make amends by feasting them all beneath her roof for a while.

All save Eurylochus were eager enough to accept, and set about beaching the ship; but Eurylochus was still like one in the grip of a nightmare, and begged them not to go, but to put to sea quickly, and escape the witch's power.

Odysseus drew his sword, minded to finish the man, friend and kinsman though he was, before he could spread his fear among the rest. But the others begged him to leave Eurylochus to keep watch on their ship while they went up to the house of the enchantress. And this Odysseus agreed to. But they had not gone far on their way when Eurylochus came after them, more afraid of being left alone than of going forward with his comrades.

So they went on together, and all together they came to Circe's house and the feast that she and her maidens had made ready for them.

THE LAND OF THE DEAD

THEY FEASTED AND SLEPT soft and feasted again, and the days passed
pleasantly enough; and no one, not even Odysseus, noticed how
they went by, for on Circe's enchanted island time seemed to
matter less than in the world of men. But when a whole year had gone
by, and the flowers that had scented the woodland clearings when first
they came that way opened their petals again, his men came to him
saying, "Lord, if ever we are to leave this place and return to our own
homes, it is time that you began to think of Ithaca once more."

So that night, when the men were sleeping as usual in the darkened
hall, Odysseus went to speak alone with Circe in her own apartments.

And Circe, combing her long dark hair, said to him, "Go then, in all
kindness. But even I cannot tell you all the things you need to know if
you are to come at last over the sea-ways to your own land."

"Who then can tell us these things?" asked Odysseus.

Still the lady Circe combed her hair. "You must go to the Land of the
Dead, to the dark halls of Hades and Persephone. There you must call up
the ghost of the blind prophet Tiresias of Thebes. He alone has the
knowledge that you need."

Then Odysseus' heart sank within him, for how should he, a living
man, go down to the Land of the Dead, and return again?

But Circe told him the ways that he must go and the things that he
must do, and gave him a black ram and a black ewe for sacrifices when
the right time came.

And next day he called his crew together, and led them down to the ship. All save one: Elpenor, the youngest of them, had got very drunk the night before, and gone to sleep by himself on the flat roof for the sake of the cool air. When the bustle of departure roused him, he came hurrying, still half-asleep, missed his footing on the ladder and fell to the ground, breaking his neck.

The rest of the crew, who had thought that they were sailing for Ithaca and their own homes, flung themselves down by the ship and wept when Odysseus told them of the dark voyage that they must make first. But there was no help in weeping, and sorrowfully they ran the ship down into the shallows and loaded the gear on board, together with the black ram and ewe. Then they set sail, and a wind sent by Circe bore them where it would.

It bore them for maybe a day and maybe many days, out of the light and into the dark, to the deep-flowing river Oceanus which girdles the earth, and on to a land that is forever cloaked in mist and never sees the sun, to the sad grove of poplars and willows that is Persephone's own. And there they beached the ship, and went on foot, following the Oceanus' banks to the place where the two rivers of the Dead come together.

There they dug out a trench, and poured into it honey mixed with milk and wine which Circe had sent with them for the purpose, praying as they did so to the ghosts of the dead. Then Odysseus sacrificed the ram and the ewe as Circe had bidden, and let their red blood run into the trench.

And the pale ghosts came, eager to sniff the blood. Shades of brides who had died long ago, and youths and unhappy old men, and warriors who had fallen in battle, their spears shadowy in their hands, their wounds still upon them. And Odysseus, with fear clamped cold in his belly, bade his men flay the sheep and burn the sacred portions to Hades and Persephone. And while they did so, he sat by the trench with his drawn sword across his knees, that no spirit before Tiresias might come at the fresh blood.

The first to come up was the shade of young Elpenor, begging Odysseus to burn his body, for until that was done he might not mingle with his fellow shades. And Odysseus promised to burn his body as soon as he returned to Circe's island. Then came the shade of his own mother, who had died since he left home, but despite his grief, he would not let even her come near the blood until Tiresias had tasted it.

And then, at last, came the shade of the blind prophet and begged Odysseus to let him drink the blood of the sacrifice; and Odysseus sheathed his sword and stood back.

When Tiresias had tasted the blood and drawn strength from it, he spoke out with the true voice of the seer. "Poseidon, Lord of the Sea, is still wroth with you for the blinding of his son, and will make your voyage a hard one. Nevertheless, you and your men may still come safe to your own landing-beach if you listen now to my warning.

"You will come in your voyaging to the island of Thrinacia, and there you will find the cattle of Hyperion the Sun Lord grazing on rich pastureland. Leave them to graze in peace, and all may yet be well with your homecoming. But harm them in any way and I see destruction for your ship and your crew; and for you, if maybe you escape the fate of your men, I see a lone homecoming in a stranger's ship to a house full of strife and sorrow. Proud men are laying waste your possessions and pressing marriage upon your wife, Penelope, who believes you long since lost to her."

"So be it, if that is what the gods decree," Odysseus said. And seeing the shade of his mother still hovering close by, he asked how he might have speech with her.

"Any shade whom you allow to come at the blood of the sacrifice will then be able to speak with you," Tiresias said. His voice grew fainter even as he spoke; and he was gone.

Then Odysseus' mother came up, and he let her taste the blood, and afterward they spoke together, and she asked what he did in that place, and told him how she had died of grief when he was so many years away. Longingly they spoke to each other, and three times Odysseus reached out to take her in his arms; but each time, like a shadow or a dream, she slipped away. And at last there was only emptiness where she had been.

Then up came more and more of the dead. Among them was Agememnon, who had been the High King and led the black ships to Troy. And when he had tasted the dark blood, he told how at his homecoming he had been slain by his wife's lover, he and all his companions, at a feast that they had thought was to welcome them back. Then he too was gone, and in his place came the mighty Ajax; and then Achilles, the greatest of them all. But Achilles said that he would sooner be the servant of a poor farmer on earth than rule over all the dead in this sad, grey land where the sun never shone and no flowers grew, save the pale asphodel. He asked for news of his friends and his kindred in the upper world; and when Odysseus had told him all he knew, he went away, walking with great strides as he had done when he was alive, and was lost in the shadows.

Many were the sights that passed before the eyes of Odysseus and his men: King Minos with his golden sceptre; and Orion the Hunter rounding up in fields of asphodel the very beasts his living hands had slain.

Tantalus they saw, burning for all time with an agony of thirst. For though he stood chin-deep in a pool of clean water, every time he bent his head to drink, the water drained away to a damp stain around his feet, and each time he reached despairingly to snatch a pear or pomegranate from the trees that overarched the pool, the wind caught their branches and tossed them high toward the clouds.

Sisyphus they saw too, the sweat pouring from him and the dust-cloud rising above his head, as he strove with bursting heart to thrust uphill the mighty boulder which, every time it reached the crest, toppled backward and rolled down again to the bottom.

Many and many were the ghosts who came, flocking thicker and thicker out of the shadows and filling the air with their wailing cries; the ghosts of all those who had died since the world began. And at last, the fear that had been rising all the while in the living men became too strong for them, and they turned and made their way back as swiftly as might be to the grove of poplars where they had left their ship.

They cast off the hawsers, and sailed from that sad shore, out of the shadows and into the sunlight; and so, riding the west wind, back to the island of Circe.

SEA PERILS

THE FIRST THING that Odysseus did, when he and his men returned to the enchantress's isle, was to see Elpenor burned and a mound piled over his ashes, and his oar set up on the crest of it for a marker.

Then they feasted with Circe as they had done so often before, and told her all that had passed since last they had feasted there. And that night, finding them still set on sailing for home, she warned Odysseus of the perils still in store, telling him how to overcome each one: the peril of the Sirens and the peril of the Wandering Rocks, and the peril of Scylla and Charybdis. And Odysseus listened, and stored up in his heart all that she told him.

At dawn they parted for the last time. Circe wandered off into the forest, while Odysseus and his crew boarded the ship and headed out once more into unknown seas.

At first they were carried along by a soft wind that was a last gift from the enchantress. But after a while the wind fell away into a breathless calm. And at the heart of the calm, an island like a flowering meadow seemed to float upon the water. And from the island drifted the sound of women's voices singing: a sound so faint that it was only on the edge of hearing, but so sweet that it seemed to draw the hearers like a silken thread. But Odysseus knew, for Circe had warned him, that these were the Sirens who sit among their flowers and sing to seamen whose ships pass by; but the flowers and the long grasses hide the bones of men who have answered their call and died of their sweet strange singing that carries the soul away.

He bade his men cease rowing – for they had taken to the oars when the wind failed – and he brought out a large lump of beeswax that Circe had given him, and cut it into small pieces which he gave to his men, bidding them stop their ears that they might not hear the singing.

But he himself hungered to hear the Siren-song, so he ordered his men to bind him to the mast with strong ropes, and not to unbind him, however much he might struggle and cry out to them, until the island was well behind them. The men did as he bade them, then returned to their rowing and sent the ship onward through the water until they were close to the shore and could see the beautiful maidens, and Odysseus could hear their sweet singing across the gentle lapping of the wavelets on the sand.

"Come nearer, Odysseus,
Flower of all Greek warriors,
Bring your ship to rest, and listen to our song.
Our voices are sweet as honey in the comb,
And all things are known to us, all things that happened before Troy,
All things that shall come to pass upon the fruitful earth . . ."

And Odysseus' heart was filled with longing, so that he struggled desperately against his binding ropes, and shouted to his comrades to cut him free, though he knew that they could not hear. But the men only quickened their oar-beat, driving the ship more swiftly through the water, till the island dropped far astern and the voices of the Sirens died away.

Then they took the wax out of their ears and unbound their captain, who was weeping as though for the loss of all the world.

And the first of Circe's perils was safely passed.

But it was not long before the next peril was upon them. Half-lost in a rolling murk of spray, two vast black rocks reared their crests toward the clouds, and between them a narrow sea-way ran like a mountain river. Close under the left-hand rock was a churning and boiling whirlpool where the sea-monster Charybdis sucked down the sea three times a day and three times vomited it up again – a whirlpool in which no ship might live. And in a cave midway up the right-hand rock another monster, Scylla by name, had her lair. She had six heads on long thin scaly necks, and in each mouth three rows of grinding teeth and twelve long feelers with claws at their ends, with which she caught her prey: big fish or dolphins – or men, if any passed that way.

All this Odysseus knew, for Circe had told him. But he knew also that the jagged reefs stretching to right and left, under a spume of breaking waves, were not rooted on the sea-bed as reefs should be, but free-moving. And if anything sought to pass among them, a ship, or even a sea-bird, they would clash together like cymbals, grinding and destroying, leaving nothing but wreckage and dead men or a few blood-stained feathers behind. For this reason, the gods called them the Wandering Rocks.

No way through, then, save between Scylla and Charybdis. And for any following that terrible sea-way the choice was between Charybdis, who could suck down a whole ship if it fell into her clutches, and Scylla, who could take only a few men at a time. Hiding the sickness in his belly, Odysseus ordered the helmsman to keep close in to the right-hand rock, but did not tell him why.

So they drove in through the narrows, keeping as close as might be to Scylla's rock, and as far as might be from the boiling and roaring and grinding turmoil of the whirlpool that sought to lay hold of them and suck them down. And as they fought their way along, out from her cave in the rock flashed the six heads of Scylla, and caught up six men from the rowing benches.

Even as they struggled and cried out to their comrades for the help that no one could give them, the men were gone into the cave darkness, and their shrieks were lost in the roaring of the waters.

Odysseus shouted to his remaining men, "Row! In the names of all the gods, row your guts out! *Row!*"

And they bent to their oars and rowed as they had never rowed before, through those dreadful narrows, and out at last into the open sea, leaving their friends behind them.

Never were men more spent and weary; and when, later, they sighted a green and gentle island and heard, even while they were still a way offshore, the bleating of sheep and the lowing of cattle, it seemed that here they would be able to take the rest they so much needed.

But Odysseus remembered the warning of Tiresias concerning the cattle of the Sun, and bade his crew row on. Then Eurylochus rebelled. He said the men could row no further; they must land and eat, and sleep onshore before they took to the sea-ways again; and the men joined with him, shouting that they must have rest. And Odysseus saw that he must yield, though first he made them swear not to touch the cattle of Hyperion.

They made the ship fast in a sheltered cove and went ashore, ate from the food-store that Circe had given them and, so weary that they forgot even their grief for lost comrades, lay down to sleep.

But in the night, Zeus the Cloud Gatherer sent a great storm. Clouds blotted out sea and sky, and the wild west wind hurled the waves upon the coast. Odysseus and his companions managed to haul the ship up clear of the breakers, into the mouth of a shallow grassy hollow which the nymphs who tended the Sun-cattle used as a dancing floor. And there they settled down to wait out the storm. But the gale raged for a whole month, and no ship might put to sea. The stores that Circe had given them were soon gone, and they lived as best they could on the few fish and sea-birds that they could catch in such weather. At last, Odysseus went up alone into the heart of the island to pray at the shrine there, to the gods of Olympus, for their aid. And when he had prayed, sleep came upon him.

When he awoke, the storm was still raging. He set out to rejoin the ship, and as he drew near the cove with its green dancing floor, the wind carried to him the sweet smell of roasting meat.

"We can but hope that the gods will have mercy on us," Eurylochus said when their captain rebuked them for their folly. "We would have starved, for sure, if we had not taken the steers, and starvation is an ill death to die."

The evil was done, and could not be undone again by going hungry, so they ate the meat of the beasts they had slaughtered, staying their bellies on it for six days.

On the sixth day the storm passed. The wind sank and the sun broke through the clouds, and they ran the ship down into the shallows and set sail, in high hopes that the Sun Lord had forgiven them for the slaughter of some of his cattle, seeing that their need for food had been so desperate.

But as soon as they were out of sight of land, a great thundercloud came climbing up the sky until it overshadowed them with a black murk, though all around the sea was sunlit blue. Then a great squall of wind leapt upon them, tearing sails and rigging and snapping off the mast, which came crashing down, striking the steersman on the head as it swept him overboard, so that he was dead before he hit the water. And from the dark heart of the stormcloud a jagged bolt of lightning whiplashed down and struck the ship, so that she staggered and reeled to the blow, filling with the stink of sulphur, and the men were flung overboard in a struggling mass.

For a while their heads bobbed like dark sea-birds on the waves. Then, one after another, they sank.

Only Odysseus remained, clinging to a rope; and as the ship broke up he hauled himself on to the mast and clung there.

The storm died down as quickly as it had risen; and the mast floated; and on the mast Odysseus, alone now of all his company, drifted for nine long days and nights.

On the tenth night, more dead than alive, he was cast up on the shore of another island. And there in the pale dawn, with the sea-birds crying, he was found lying like a frond of sea-wrack stranded on the tide-line by the nymph Calypso, the lady of the island.

TELEMACHUS SEEKS HIS FATHER

FOR SEVEN LONG YEARS Odysseus remained on Calypso's island; it was far from the sea-ways by which ships pass to and fro, and he had no means of building a ship of his own, nor any rowers for it if he could have built one. And Calypso, who was very kind to him in all other ways, could not bring herself to help him on his homeward voyaging, for her heart longed for him to stay with her always and be her lover.

But all Odysseus longed for was the sight of rocky Ithaca and the smoke rising from his own hearth.

And so the years went by.

Meanwhile in Ithaca, there was sorrow and to spare for his wife Penelope, and for Telemachus their son, who had been little more than a babe when the black ships sailed for Troy. For as the years went by and nothing more was heard of Odysseus, everyone supposed that he must be dead. That was when his mother died of grief. And after her death his father Laertes, who was still alive and should have been ruling the kingdom while his son was at war (for in Ithaca, sons and fathers shared the kingship as they sometimes did in Egypt), became a sick old man, and went to spend his last years on his farm in the country. Telemachus was still a boy, so there was no strong hand to rule in Ithaca. And the young men who had been boys when the black ships sailed had grown up into an unruly mob. They did whatever they were minded to do in all things, and they were minded, each and every one, to wed Penelope and through her seize the kingdom, though of course Telemachus was the rightful heir.

They descended upon the palace like a flock of greedy gulls. They slew the king's cattle and drank the king's wine, and swore that they would not leave until the queen should choose one of them for her husband. And no one could make them go.

At last, to hold them off for a while, Penelope promised that she would make her choice when she had finished the fine linen web that she was weaving to be a shroud for old Laertes when he died. All day long she worked at her loom, but each night, when the young lords her suitors were sleeping in their own homes or in the palace outhouses, she undid all the work that she had done that day, so the cloth never came any nearer to being finished. For a while, that kept the young men at bay; but eventually one of the women slaves who had a grudge against her betrayed her secret, and so she had no choice left but to finish her weaving. Even so, she tried desperately to put off making her choice of husband from one day to another. But her suitors clamoured more roughly than ever, and the time was coming when she would be forced to yield.

At last, bright-eyed Pallas Athene, goddess of wisdom, who had always favoured Odysseus, looked down from high Olympus and saw what was happening, and she spoke to the other gods on his behalf. She told them how he was held captive by Calypso, and how the nymph tried to make him forget his own land and people in the hope that he would grow to love her instead; but how he longed for them still, while other men wasted his wealth and sought to steal his wife. She told them that she herself would go to Ithaca and persuade Telemachus that he was now old enough to take matters in hand. Meanwhile, let Hermes go at once to Calypso and tell her that, however much Odysseus' loss might grieve her, the gods decreed that the time had come when she must let him go free and set him on his way.

In the end, Athene won them over, all save Poseidon. But Poseidon was away in Ethiopia on some matter concerning mortal men.

So she flashed down like a shooting star to Ithaca, where she took the shape of an old friend of Odysseus, Mentes by name, that she might walk easily among men. And in that guise she went to the palace.

In the great foreporch she found the young men sitting on the hides of oxen that they had slaughtered for meat, playing knucklebones, while the servants made ready the evening meal. Telemachus, who was standing apart as though he had no right in the doorway of his own house, saw the stranger, bade him welcome and led him into the great hall, never guessing that in truth his guest was the goddess Athene.

And when the suitors came swaggering in and descended on the tables where the evening meal was spread, he drew the stranger aside and seated him at a small table where he might eat in peace. And when the servants had brought food, he told him, speaking softly that none of the suitors might hear, the meaning of the ill-mannered mob in his father's hall, and how he feared that his father must be long since dead; and asked the stranger his name and what brought him there.

Athene, still in the guise of the chieftain Mentes, told Telemachus that she was an old friend of Odysseus, and had touched at Ithaca on the way to Cyprus to buy copper, thinking to find him already there, for he was certainly alive and on his way home. And seeing the hope kindle in Telemachus' face, she bade him gather an assembly of the Ithacan people and complain to them of the suitors; then order a ship to be made ready for sea, and himself go seeking the latest news of his father.

Then she departed, leaving Telemachus to feel his spirit growing strong in him for the first time.

Next day, the young prince called the assembly and spoke to the people as a grown man and his father's son. But he might have saved himself the trouble, for from the suitors he had only jibes and insults, while the rest of the people, though they sorrowed for him and the evil state of things, felt that there was nothing they could do.

That evening Athene came again, still in the guise of his father's friend, and with her encouragement Telemachus ordered a twenty-oar galley to be made ready for sea, and told the suitors openly that he was away to seek tidings of his father from the kings Nestor and Menelaus. But he did not tell his mother, and it was old Eurycleia, who had been his nurse and his father's before him, who brought him food and wine for the journey from the king's storerooms, to which she had the key.

And at night, when Athene sent them a following wind singing over the wine-dark sea, they sailed from Ithaca.

But meanwhile the suitors, furious and frightened, were making a plot to be rid of Telemachus once and for all. "Give me a ship and a crew of twenty," said Antinous, one of the leaders among them, "and I'll lie up for him between Ithaca and the bluffs of Same and catch him on his homeward way, and a harsh ending there'll be to this sea-jaunting in search of his father!"

And so it was agreed between them.

At noon next day, Telemachus and his rowers beached their ship below sandy Pylos, the city of Nestor. The old king gave him warm welcome, but could tell him no more of his father than he knew already; and the day after, he was on his way again, in a chariot from the royal stables, with Pisistratus, one of the king's sons who had fought at Troy, for his charioteer. And late on the second day of driving, the steep hill-tracks brought them down to the cornlands of Sparta, and as night fell they clattered into the outer court of the fortress palace of Menelaus.

Now Menelaus, and Helen with him, had also had long and weary sea-wanderings after leaving Troy, and were only lately returned to their own land. And the king was feasting with his companions, glad of their homecoming, when Telemachus and Pisistratus arrived. He did not ask who they were, for to do so before they had eaten and drunk would have been discourteous. But he ordered hot water and fresh raiment to be made ready for them, and when they had bathed and changed their clothes, he summoned them to join him at his own table.

When the meal was over, into the hall from her own chamber came Helen of the Fair Cheeks, beautiful as ever she had been, and behind her two of her bower-maidens carrying her golden spindle and her silver distaff loaded with wool of the deepest violet colour. She sat down at her lord's knee, and as she took up her spinning, her gaze went across the hearth and touched upon the face of Telemachus. And leaning aside toward Menelaus, she asked, "Oh my lord, have you yet asked our guests their names and where they come from?"

"Not yet," said the king. "I had thought maybe to leave the asking until they have had a night's rest, for they are weary with wayfaring."

"I think that I can answer for one of them without waiting for the morning," said Helen, smiling at the strangers. "It is in my mind that the younger is Telemachus, son of our old and dear friend Odysseus. Oh my lord, do you not see the likeness?"

And Menelaus, looking more closely than he had done before, exclaimed, "I do indeed see the likeness – and I scarce know whether to rejoice or weep or both together!"

Telemachus, not used to strangers, flushed like a girl, and could say nothing at all. But Pisistratus spoke up for him, saying that he was indeed Odysseus' son and had come seeking news of his father, while he himself was Pisistratus, son of Nestor, and had come with Telemachus to bear him company. Then they all rejoiced and wept together, and Helen told how Odysseus had come to her house disguised as a beggar when he came to steal away the Luck of Troy. And Menelaus told of Odysseus' invention of the Wooden Horse, which in the end had gained them the city.

But it grew late, and nothing more was said that night as to where Odysseus might be now, or the chance that he was still alive.

Next day, Telemachus told his host all that there was to tell of the state of things in Ithaca, of his mother's sorrows, and of the suitors who, believing his father dead, sought to force themselves upon her; and how, being told by a passing copper merchant that his father yet lived, he had come to Menelaus to ask if he had any word of him or where he might be.

"Some of what you ask I can tell you," said Menelaus, "a strange story – the gods grant that it be true. In my wanderings after I left Troy, I found myself in Cyprus and Egypt and Phoenicia, even in Libya on the north coast of Africa. And not much more than a year ago, storm winds held me for close on a moon on Pharos, a day's voyage from the mouth of the Nile. We were almost starving, for all our stores were gone. But on that island lives a goddess, daughter to Proteus, the Old Man of the Sea; and, taking pity on us, she came to me when I was walking apart from my men, and told me that only her father could tell me how to make my peace with the gods so that they would send me a fair wind. Each day at noon, he was used to come out to sleep on the shore with all his company of seals about him; and if I could catch and hold him (for he would turn into all manner of terrible shapes as he tried to break free), he would return to his own shape at last, and then he must answer whatever I asked him.

"The goddess dug shallow trenches in the sand for me and three of my men, and covered us with the shed skins of seals. And there we waited.

"At noon, the Old Man came ashore with his seals, and lay down to sleep on the wave-patterned sand. When he was asleep, we leapt out upon him and held him with all our strength. He turned into a lion and a boar, a leopard and a snake, into running water, into a tall flowering tree. But we clung on, and at last he fell back into his own shape. Then he told me what I asked: that I should not have a fair wind until I returned to the Nile mouth, and made the sacrifice to all the gods that I should have made before setting out. And then, when I asked for word of friends and kindred, he told me how my brother Agamemnon had been slain in his own hall. That evil story you will know already. And lastly he told me of Odysseus, how he was held captive on a far-off island by the nymph Calypso, for the love she bore him.

"Seven years he has passed on her island," said Menelaus, bringing his tale to an end, "longing always for his own land and his own people. But no ships pass that way."

"How may I find that island?" Telemachus asked, almost before Menelaus had done speaking.

"There is no way," said the king. "But I think that the gods would not have been at such great pains to keep him yet living – him alone, as it seems, of all his company – if they did not mean that he should reach home at last."

And with that Telemachus had to be content.

FAREWELL TO CALYPSO

WHILE TELEMACHUS WAS still at the court of Menelaus, the gods sent Hermes as their messenger to the nymph Calypso. He bound his winged sandals to his feet, and down he flew to her island; and landing before the cave where she lived, he found her within, weaving at her loom with a shuttle of purest gold and singing as she tossed it to and fro. There was a fire on the hearth, and the cave was full of the scent of burning cedar and sandalwood. Alder and poplar and sweet-smelling cyprus trees grew round about, their branches alive with falcons and horned owls. A vine dripping with the dark sweetness of grapes trailed over the cave entrance, and four clear springs watered the flowery meadow spread below. Surely there could be no more pleasant place for a man to be held captive.

But when Hermes looked within the cave, Odysseus was not there. He was away on the lonely headland where he spent his days, as he had spent them for seven long years, looking out to sea for a sail which he knew would never come, his heart sick with longing for his own hills.

Calypso left her weaving when the god entered, and welcomed him in and seated him in a chair spread with a shining cloth, and set nectar and ambrosia, the food and drink of the gods, before him.

"Hermes of the Golden Rod," said she, "no one could be more welcome here than you, but tell me what brings you this way, for it is not often that you come to my door. Is there something that you would have me do? Tell me, and if it may be done, then I will gladly do it. But first, eat and take your rest."

And when he had eaten, Hermes told her the reason for his coming. "It is Zeus the All-Father himself who sends me here, and my errand concerns the man Odysseus, one of the heroes who fought nine years at Troy, and whom you have here with you in this place. On their way home, he and his ships' crews earned the wrath of Poseidon, and then of Hyperion the Sun Lord, and the two gods raised against them storms and all manner of disasters in revenge. Every man of his company was lost; and he himself, alone and desolate, the winds and waves cast upon your shore. And for seven of what mortal men call years you have kept him here with you. Now mighty Zeus bids you set him free and send him on his way. For it is not his fate to live and die here, far from all his friends."

Then Calypso began to shake like a poplar tree with grief and anger. "You are hard!" she cried. "Hard and jealous, all you gods who dwell upon Olympus and never feel the cold rain or the sorrows of the world! I found him helpless upon the shore and took him in; and I have loved and cherished him all this while. I would have made him immortal if he would have taken that gift from me. Now I must let him go; so be it. That is the ruling of the gods, and I must obey. But how shall I help him on his way, seeing that I have no ship and no rowers? Yet I will tell him he is free to go, and give him whatever help I may."

"Do that, and swiftly," said Hermes, "as swiftly as may be, lest Zeus feel himself kept waiting, and grow wroth with you."

And he was gone from beside her hearth.

Then Calypso went sadly down to the shore, and found Odysseus in his usual place, sitting on a rock with his head in his hands, and gazing out to sea with eyes bleary and red with weeping. She touched him lightly on the shoulder. "No more weeping and wasting your life away in this place," she said. "The time has come for me to set you on your way, back to your own hearth and the woman who sits beside it. And since I must do this at the bidding of the gods whether I will or no, I will do it in kindness and with my whole heart."

But Odysseus lifted his heavy head and said, "Though you set me free, how am I to leave this place?"

"Build for yourself a boat with the tools and timber that I shall give you," said Calypso. "I will put bread and water and wine on board, and give you a fair wind to carry you home." And she sighed, deeply and sorrowfully. "Yet, if you knew what evils you must endure before you sit in peace beside your own hearth once more, I think that you might well choose to remain with me, even though by doing so you would not again see the wife whom I know you long for day by day."

"Do not be angry with me for that," Odysseus said. "Well I know that Penelope has not your beauty – what mortal woman could shine like the immortals? But even so, I long to return to her, as you say. And as for the troubles and dangers of the voyage if I should come again to shipwreck, I must endure it as I have done before, taking my chance with the sea and all its perils."

Next day, Calypso brought him the tools of a carpenter, and showed him the best trees to use; and he felled twenty of them close to the shore, and built a wide shallow boat, using the tallest and straightest fir tree for a mast. She brought him fine linen canvas, and he made a sail. She brought him hides, and he cut them into strips and plaited the strips into ropes and halyards. In four days all was finished, and on the fifth he set rollers beneath the hull and urged it down into the shallows.

Calypso put on board skins full of wine and water and meal, and gave Odysseus stout garments for the voyage. Then they kissed each other in farewell, and she turned back alone to her cave, while Odysseus headed out to sea, his sails swelling with the fair wind that she had promised him.

So long as the fair wind lasted, Odysseus held his place at the steering oar, never seeing land or any other ship. By day he steered by the sun, and at night he steered by the stars, keeping the Great Bear always on his left, as Calypso had bidden him. And so he sailed for seventeen days; and on the eighteenth day he saw far off the faint shadow of mountain peaks that he thought he recognised.

But, just as it seemed that he was drawing near to the familiar world and the end of his troubles, blue-haired Poseidon, on his way back from Ethiopia, saw him and knew that the other gods had gone behind his back to aid the man who had blinded his son. And in anger he raised a mighty storm. Black clouds rolled across the sky and the winds swooped in from all quarters, buffeting the boat among them. Then came a white squall from the north. It broke off the mast, and sail and yard-arm went into the sea; and Odysseus, his hands torn from the steering oar, went overboard in the same instant.

The pressure of the waves sent him down and down, and the weight of the garments that Calypso had given him was like to be his death. But he fought his way up to the surface at last, gasping for air and spitting out salt brine. And swimming after what remained of his boat, he managed to climb back amidships, while the wind and waves tossed him about like a seagull's feather.

But while he clung there, a sea-goddess, Ino by name, saw his desperate plight and came up through the wild waters to his aid, breaking the wave-crest beside him like a sea-mew coming up from its dive. She threw her shining veil to him, saying, "Strip off those garments, which will only weigh you down, and bind this around your waist; it will keep you from harm. Then leave the boat and swim for the land that you have already seen; and when you reach the shore, cast my veil back into the waters, turning your head towards the land."

And she was gone, back into the deeps whence she had come.

In that instant a mountainous wave hurtled down, scattering the timbers of the boat. Odysseus scrambled on to one of the beams and sitting astride it, dragged off his sodden clothes and bound the veil about his waist. Then he flung himself into the water and began to swim. And now bright-eyed Athene came to his aid, quenching all the winds except the wind from the north that would help him toward the distant land.

For two days and nights Athene's north wind carried him in the right direction. On the third day the land was very near, and the wind sank to a flat calm, and Odysseus began to swim for the rocky shore. But soon he was engulfed in a terrible surf that crashed and pounded on the rocks; and he would have been broken like a bit of driftwood, but that he managed to grasp a jagged rock-spur and cling to it until the savage backwash dragged him out again. Three times he clung to the rock, and three times he was dragged out again by the undertow. And at last he gave up trying to land there, and struck out along the coast outside the line of breakers looking for a better place, until he came to quieter water where a broad river flowed into the sea, and his feet found shelving sand.

He staggered clear of the water and up the beach, pitched forward on his face and knew no more for a while.

When he came back to himself, he unbound Ino's veil from his waist and flung it far out, turning his head away as she had bidden him. He pushed inland a little way, following the bank of the river. But he had not the strength to get far. When he came to two ancient and twisted olive trees growing close together, whose crowding stems and interwoven branches made a shelter from the wind, he crept between them, and finding the ground there thick with fallen leaves, covered himself with them until a faint warmth stirred in him. And Athene closed his eyes in sleep.

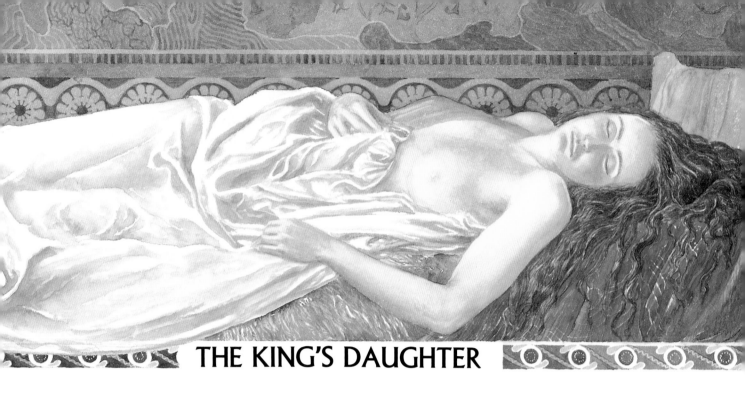

THE KING'S DAUGHTER

Now, WHILE ODYSSEUS slept under his covering of olive leaves on the river bank, up in the high palace of the king of that country the Princess Nausicaa slept also. And in her sleep, Pallas Athene came to her in the guise of a friend of hers, a sea-captain's daughter.

She stood beside the bed, seeming half-vexed and half-laughing, saying, "Nausicaa, how does your mother come to have such a heedless daughter? Look at all the beautiful clothes you leave lying about neglected, though you may soon be married – you with every young noble in the land in love with you – and have need of them for your marriage-chest and for guest-presents! Let us go down to the river and do some washing in the morning, with a cart to carry the garments."

When she woke in the morning, Nausicaa remembered what she thought was her dream; and she went to her father the king and asked him for a mule-cart, that she might take her linen down to the river for washing.

And her father lent her a smooth-running cart with a pair of mules harnessed to it. The servants piled in the bright-coloured garments, and the queen her mother caused food and wine to be packed in also, and gave her a flask of the softest olive oil, that she and her maidens might go bathing and anoint themselves afterwards. And Nausicaa climbed into the cart and took up the reins and drove off toward the river, not too fast, because of all her maidens following on foot.

They came to the river and to the clear shallow pool that was the best place for washing clothes; and there they turned the mules loose to graze. Then they began to wash the garments they had brought, treading them down in the water-slides over the broad stones, and, when they were rinsed clean, spreading them out to dry in the sun and wind along the bank.

While the clothes dried, the girls bathed and rubbed themselves with olive oil and, pulling on their loose tunics again, feasted on the fruit and little cakes and honeyed wine that the queen had sent with them.

When they had eaten their fill they began to play with a ball of gilded leather, tossing it from one to another and singing as they played, Nausicaa leading the round-song. As they played, Athene of the Shining Eyes joined in the game unseen, and when Nausicaa threw the ball to one of her maidens running by, she caused it to miss the girl and fall into the eddying currents of the river. Then all the maidens set up such a laughing and shrieking that the noise they made woke Odysseus from his sleep between the olive trees, scarce a spear-throw downstream.

For a few heartbeats of time he lay still, half-roused, and thinking by the screams that some nearby village was being attacked by an enemy, or a cruel master was beating his women slaves. But as he woke more fully, the sounds changed in his ears to the squealing of girls at play. Maybe if he asked them, they would give him the help he so sorely needed. He hauled himself to his knees, then to his feet, and, breaking off a branch of wild olive to cover his nakedness, he dragged himself slowly and stiffly out from the riverside scrub.

But his feet were bare and bleeding and his face wild with all that he had suffered, and his matted hair and beard rimed with sea-salt. To the playing girls he looked as fearsome as a lion breaking out of a thicket, and they screamed in good earnest and ran this way and that, all save the Princess Nausicaa, who stood and awaited his coming with wide grave eyes.

And Odysseus, not daring to come close and touch her knees in entreaty, checked and spoke to her from a little distance. "Oh young mistress, are you goddess or mortal maiden? If you are a goddess, then surely you must be Artemis of the Crescent Moon. If you are mortal, then lucky indeed are your father and your gentle mother, and lucky your brothers also. How their hearts must lift each time they see their darling join the dance! But most happy of all must be the man whose love and wedding gifts win you to his home! Never have I seen such perfection save once – on Delos, a young palm sapling springing beside the altar of Apollo. Yet it is not your beauty but your kindness that I appeal to, for it is only yesterday, after many days storm-tossed on the sea, that some god cast me upon this shore, not knowing where I am or what more of ill fortune may wait for me. Of your mercy, give me an old garment to put on, and tell me how to find the nearest town. And may the gods grant you a husband whose heart and mind are one with yours in a happy house."

"Stranger, you do not seem an evil man, and certainly, to judge by your words, you are a gently-mannered one," said the princess. "It is doubtless the will of Zeus, who sends joy and sorrow to each man as he chooses, that has brought you to our shores. And being here, you shall indeed have a garment to cover yourself, and I will lead you to the city, with good welcome, for I am the daughter of Alcinous, the king of this island which is called Phaeacia."

Then she called to her maidens, who had checked their flight and were hovering at a little distance all about her. "What is there to fear, my maids? Surely not the sight of this poor stranger? Do you not know that no enemy ever comes our way, dear to the gods as we are, and islanded in the far-most wash of the waves, where the ships of the world never pass by? This is a wanderer brought here by sad mischance; come close now, and bring him a garment for his nakedness."

So, timidly at first, the girls returned. They brought Odysseus to a loop of the river-bank where crowding alder trees gave shelter from the wind, and gave him a mantle from among the newly-dried clothes, and the oil that remained in the bottom of the queen's flask, and bade him wash off the salt sea-harshness.

Odysseus thanked them for the mantle and the oil, but asked them to leave him. "For," said he, "I do not like to cast off even this poor garment of green leaves and take my bath before ladies."

So they left him and went to tell the princess. And Odysseus washed himself in the sweet water below the bank, rinsing the brine from his body and salt-scurfed head, and rubbed the oil into his skin that had not known its gentleness for many a long day. Into his head, too, he rubbed the oil, until his hair curled close about it like the petals of the hyacinth flower. Then he put on the mantle that the maidens had given him, and went up from the water's edge and sat down on the bank.

And Nausicaa, glancing from afar, saw him sitting there clean and clad, and beautiful in her eyes. And she said longingly to her maidens, "Could it indeed be the will of some god that cast him up here on our shore? When first I saw him I thought him ugly. But now – surely the gods themselves could not be more fair! I wish that it might please him to bide here and become my marriage-lord . . . But come, this is no time for dreaming. Let us bring him food and drink."

So they brought Odysseus all that was left of the summer feast that the queen had sent with them. And while he ate and drank, eagerly, for he had gone hungry for many days, they gathered up the garments that the sun and wind had dried for them, and loaded them into the cart and harnessed up the mules.

When all was ready for the return, and Odysseus had finished eating, the princess climbed into the cart and took up the reins as before. Then she called to Odysseus, and when he came and stood beside the wheel, she told him, "It is time that you come to my father's house. Listen now, and do as I say, and all shall turn out well. So long as we are in the farm-lands, keep with my maidens behind the cart. But when we draw near to the city, and reach the place where there is a fair haven with shipyards on either side of the way, turn aside from us into the grove of poplars sacred to Athene that grow there, and wait awhile, that we may enter the city and come first to the palace. For it will not please my father to hear it said on all sides that the Princess Nausicaa has been fishing and brought home a man with her!

"When you judge that the time has been long enough, then come you into the city, and anyone will tell you the way to the palace. My father's gates stand at all times open and unguarded, so enter freely, and when you reach our shady courts and halls, make your way to the great chamber.

"There by the hearth my mother will be sitting at this time of day, spinning yarn of shining sea-purple, with her maidens all about her. There also is my father's great chair close beside her, but if he be sitting in it, pass him by, and kneel to my mother and clasp her knees and beg her for help – even a ship to carry you to your own country – for if you win her heart towards you, she will give it."

Odysseus made her a courteous bowing of the head. "All that you tell me, that I will surely do."

Then Nausicaa flicked the mules with her whip, and they moved forward, the cart lurching at their heels, and Odysseus with all the maidens following on behind.

The sun was close to setting when they reached the grove of poplar trees; and there Odysseus turned aside. There was a shrine at the heart of the grove and kneeling, he prayed to Pallas Athene that the Phaeacians might receive him in friendship. Then, when he judged that his wait had been long enough, he rose and made his way into the city.

In the city gateway Athene herself met him in the guise of a young maiden carrying a pitcher; and Odysseus asked her the way to the king's palace. "For," said he, "I am a stranger here, come from a distant land and struck by misfortune on my journeying."

"I will guide you on your way," Athene said. "Follow me, but do not try to speak with anyone in the street. Poseidon has made them a sailor folk, but they have little love for strangers who come under their own sail from other lands beyond the seas."

So saying, she turned and led the way, Odysseus following at her heels. And no man remembered afterwards having seen him pass, for the goddess had flung a mist of unseeing about him. She brought him to the king's gatehouse and pointed him to pass through, and when he looked toward her she was no longer there.

Inside the gates, Odysseus paused for a few moments. The palace gardens were rich with fruit trees, pears and pomegranates and apples with the fruit shining among their leaves, olives and figs and loaded vines, all watered by springs whose silvery trickling mingled with the song of birds. But the beauty of the garden would not help him on his way home.

Ahead of him he saw a broad white building of many colonnades and courtyards that must be the royal house; and he made his way to it and went in. And still no one saw him pass.

In the great hall the king and his chiefs and councillors were at supper, the queen and her maidens sitting by.

Up the hall he went, and knelt down at the queen's knee; and as he did so, Athene's mist of unseeing wafted away, and a startled silence came upon the crowded hall as men saw a stranger suddenly in their midst. And in the silence Odysseus made his plea to the queen.

"Royal lady, I come before you, a stranger storm-driven to these shores, begging your aid and a ship to carry me back to my own land, for it is a long and evil time since last I sat beside my home hearth."

"Poor man! If we may know your name and what land it is that you are come from –" the queen began gently.

But Alcinous the king said, "Any stranger is welcome beneath my roof. Eat before you answer our questions, and later speed safely on your way."

So Odysseus was seated on a polished chair, and maidens brought water for him to rinse his hands, and the carver set the choicest slices of meat before him with fine bread and fruit and wine. And he feasted among the rest, rejoicing in the food despite the sorrow at his heart, for the princess' cakes had done little more than blunt the edge of his hunger.

At last the feasting was over and the guests had gone to their own homes. Odysseus was left alone with Alcinous and Arete the queen in the great hall.

The queen was first to break the silence. "Stranger, now that you have eaten and rested a little, forgive me if I ask again who you are and where you come from, and how you come to be wearing that mantle which I know well, for it was woven here in the palace."

So Odysseus told how he had been driven off course on his way home from Troy, and how he had been held seven years by the nymph Calypso, until at last she had set him free and allowed him to build a rough boat. How Poseidon for an ancient grudge he bore him had wrecked his boat. And how at last he had been cast up here on the coast of Phaeacia and, falling instantly asleep in his exhaustion, he had woken to find the princess and her maidens playing close by. How he had begged her for help and she had given him the mantle from those which they had been washing, and food and drink, and oil to rub himself after he had bathed, and told him how to come to her father's house.

"One fault I find with my daughter in all this," said the king. "She should have brought you home with her, not left you to find your stranger's way alone. She was, after all, the first person whom you turned to for aid, and your welfare was in her hands."

"Nay, do not blame her for that," Odysseus said quickly. "She did bid me follow among her maidens. But it is so long since I have been among mortal women that I am somewhat shy in their company. Also, I thought that you might be ill pleased to see her returning with a strange man at her cart-tail. The fathers of fair daughters are a jealous folk."

Alcinous smiled, looking his guest up and down. "I do not think that I am of the jealous kind. To a stranger such as you would seem to be, I could even think of giving my daughter in marriage, if you were willing to forget this long voyage to some far distant home, and bide here with us in the house that I would build for the two of you." For he clearly saw that this stranger who had not yet told his name was of noble blood, and wise and strong enough to hold a wife at his hearth. Then, seeing a shadow on the stranger's face and the distant look in his eyes, he said, "But if your heart is set beyond all changing on returning to your own land, then assuredly a ship shall be made ready for you, manned by the best rowers in my kingdom."

"All that, we can speak of tomorrow," said Arete the queen. "Now it is the time for sleep." And she gave orders to her maids to make him a place to sleep with rugs and soft pillows in the inner portico.

And there Odysseus slept all night under a purple covering.

THE PHAEACIAN GAMES

NEXT DAY, ALCINOUS sent word to his people to prepare a ship for sea and have her moored in readiness at the main jetty below the town.

At midday, the chiefs and captains dined with him in the great hall of the palace. And there, while they ate, the king's bard sang to them: a man whom the gods had made sightless, as men blind a singing bird to add sweetness to the song. Striking his harp in time to the winged words, he sang of the heroes of Troy; and, listening in his seat beside the king, Odysseus pulled a fold of his mantle over his head, as men do in wild weather or when they wish to shield their faces from the gaze of those about them. But Alcinous, being closest to him, knew that he wept; and when the song was finished, rose and said that they had had enough of feasting and harp-song, and should go now to amuse themselves with running and wrestling and suchlike sports in the open air.

So they got up from the tables and went out to the gathering-place below the palace. The young men hurried to join them, among them the king's three sons; and they fell to racing and wrestling, the long jump and throwing the discus. Then the thought came to them that their guest,

who despite being worn down by hardship was built like a wrestler, might care to join them; and Laodamas, one of the king's sons, came to him with their invitation.

But Odysseus shook his head, saying that he was too heavy at heart for such games.

At that, some of the young men took offence, and one, Euryalus by name, laughed sneeringly, "Our apologies, sir. It is clear that you are a trader, captain of some sow-bellied merchant ship. It was a foolish mistake to think you might be an athlete."

At this, Odysseus' head went up and his brows drew together. "Yet I have been one in happier times, before I grew old and tired with war and wandering," he said. "And it may be, after all, that something of that yet remains to me. Shall we put it to the test?" And getting up, without even troubling to fling aside his mantle, he picked up the largest and heaviest of the great bronze discs from where they lay and, whirling about, sent it spinning from his hand. The crowd watched the shining arc that it made against the sky, and ran out to mark the spot where it pitched to earth, far ahead of any other throw that had been made that day.

Then Odysseus, his blood running light and roused within him, challenged any man there to box or wrestle or shoot at a mark with him. But Alcinous, perhaps not wishing to see his young men worsted at every sport in turn, courteously refused the challenge. "Let us show you a skill which is ours above all the world," he said, and called for the blind bard once more to make music for dancing. A wide circle was cleared, and the bard took his stand in the midst of it, while the best dancers gathered about him; and he set their feet moving on the sacred floor in time to a love song of Ares and Aphrodite that he made as light as a summer breeze. Then two of the dancers took a shining ball and began tossing it to each other as they danced, leaping high and throwing while in mid-air, and catching again at the next leap, making the air seem alive as with the darting of swallows, while the rest stood round stamping to keep time.

"This is indeed a skill in which you have no equal. Never did I see the like!" said Odysseus.

When the dancing was over, Alcinous spoke to his chieftains gathered about him, saying that each of them should make their stranger-guest a gift of gold and fine garments before he boarded the ship that waited for him; and that Euryalus should make a gift also, by way of atonement for his ill manners during the games. And this they gladly agreed to do.

The king himself gave a massive cup of worked gold, and a rich mantle and tunic of the queen's own weaving, which Arete packed together in a beautiful coffer of sweet-scented wood; and the chiefs in turn all brought their gifts for carrying down to the ship. Last of all, Euryalus brought a bronze sword with a silver hilt and a sheath of age-darkened ivory, and set it in Odysseus' hands, saying with all courtesy, "Stranger, I salute you. If I spoke harsh words to you, may the storm-winds blow them away, and may the gods bring you safely and swiftly to your own landing-beach."

"I return your greeting," Odysseus said, "and accept your atonement gift. May the gods bless you, and may you never feel the lack of the good blade that you have given me." And he slung the strap of the beautiful weapon over his shoulder.

Then, the time drawing on toward supper, the palace maidens took him to the bath, and when he had washed himself in the herb-scented water that they had heated for him, he put on the fresh garments that they had laid ready. As he made his way back to the hall, he met the princess Nausicaa standing beside a pillar that upheld the roof of the colonnade. It was the first time that they had spoken to each other since they had left the riverside, for in that country it was not the custom for unmarried maidens to eat in hall with the men. And it was to be the last time, also.

"Fare you well, my stranger," said the princess, a little sadly. "Fair winds carry you on your way. Do not forget me too quickly or too easily in your own country."

"In my own country, if indeed I come there," Odysseus told her, "I will remember you for the rest of my days; for it is you, gentle lady, who gave me back my life."

And he went on into the hall and took his place at the feasting, beside Alcinous the king.

Again the bard took his harp and played as they feasted. This time he sang of the Wooden Horse, and how the cunning and resourceful Odysseus had caused it to be built and then brought, unsuspected, into Troy; and of the picked band of warriors, Odysseus among them, hidden in its belly, who had crept out in the night and opened to their comrades the gates of the city.

And again, listening to him, Odysseus wept for the sorrows of the siege and the loss of so many friends and sword-companions.

Once more the king saw his grief, and checked the singer with a gift of sizzling boar meat, a thick slice cut from his own portion as a sign of honour. And to the stranger at his side, he said, "I notice that all songs telling of the siege of Troy give you much pain. Have you lost a kinsman or a close friend to the Trojan spears?"

"Many," said the stranger. "For I am Odysseus, son of Laertes, Lord of Ithaca. And of the twelve galley crews that went with me to the siege, I am the only man now left."

A gasp ran round the hall, and a long silence after it, as all men sat gazing at the guest in their midst; for all of them had heard of him in story and harp-song, as they had heard of ancient heroes and the gods themselves.

The king was first to break the silence. "Then Odysseus, son of Laertes, I pray you tell us of the wanderings that have brought you here, for it has been said this long while past, that Odysseus was lost on his way home from Troy, for nothing has been heard of him since his ships left the main fleet."

So, sitting there in the midst of the feasting, and far on into the night, Odysseus told the whole story of his wanderings. He told of the Cyclops, of Circe and his voyage to the underworld, of Scylla and Charybdis, the cattle of the Sun and the loss of his remaining ships; and how he came at last to Calypso's island, where the story caught up with what he had told them already.

Before dawn, the feasting and the storytelling being over, all the treasure of gold and rich garments was carried down by torchlight to the waiting ships and stowed beneath the rowing benches.

Odysseus took his leave of the king and queen, who had come down to see him on his way. To Arete the queen, as he gave the journey-cup back into her hands, he said, "My queen, good fortune to you all your life, until old age and death come to you as they come to all mortal kind. May your house be blessed and may you be happy in your children and your people and in Alcinous your lord."

Then he went on board and laid himself down wrapped in warm cloaks and rugs, while the rowers thrust off the galley, then settled to their oars and sent her forward through the parting waters to far-off Ithaca.

RETURN TO ITHACA

WHEN ODYSSEUS WOKE from the long deep sleep that Athene had cast upon him, he found himself alone, lying under an olive tree and still wrapped in the warm cloaks in which he had lain down on board Alcinous' galley; and all his rich gifts stacked about him. A thick morning mist spread by the bright-eyed goddess blotted out the shapes of the land, that he might not know himself back on his own island and start out for his home before she could warn him of what was happening there. So he thought that the Phaeacians had set him ashore in some strange place. And he checked over his treasure, drawing out the silver-hilted sword to sling over his shoulder, and fell to pacing up and down the shore while he thought of what he should do next.

And there, on the seemingly empty tide-line, Pallas Athene came to meet him in the guise of a young man, clad in a double mantle such as kings and nobles wore, and carrying a spear in his hand.

"The greeting of the morning to you," said Odysseus, not knowing her. "I pray you, tell me what land is this? Are the people friendly in these parts?"

"Truly," said Athene, "you are simple in the head to ask such a question. This is the island of Ithaca, whose name is known even as far afield as Troy."

Then a great joy woke in Odysseus at finding himself back in his own land. But he had been long away, and had no way of knowing what kind of men the children of nineteen years ago had grown into, or what kind of greeting they would have for him. Maybe a new king sat in his place, who might not even be his son.

So he did not tell the young man who he was, but said he was a Cretan. And then, to explain how a man of Crete came to be on Ithaca with his treasure stacked round him under an olive tree, and yet not know where he was, he launched into one of his long and detailed stories, telling how in Crete one of the king's sons had tried to rob him of the rich spoils of war that he had brought back from Troy. How in the fight for it he had slain the prince, and how in fear for his own life he had gathered up his treasure and escaped on board a trading ship of the Phoenicians, who had promised to put him ashore at Pylos. But the wind had blown them off course, and they had landed and slept here, and in the morning must have gone on their way, leaving him still asleep.

At this, the young man laughed. And in that instant he was gone, and in his place stood bright-eyed Athene, stately and beautiful.

"Oh, the cleverness of Odysseus!" said she, mocking. "Yet you did not know me, who have so often helped you before Troy and again in the land of King Alcinous!"

Odysseus gave her a straight look, eye to eye. "But not when I had sore need of help during my times of hideous danger at sea. Then how may I be sure that you now stand my friend? How can I even be sure that I have indeed returned to my own island?"

Athene said, "How could I go against my father's brother Poseidon, Lord of the Sea, whose wrath was hot against you for the blinding of his son? But all that is past. Now you stand upon your own shore, and I am free to help you as I will. Look about you and you will see that this is indeed your island!"

As she spoke, the grey cloud all about them rolled away as morning mist is drawn up by the sun, and Odysseus saw the familiar shapes of the land he knew and loved: the curve of the bay within its headlands, the wooded upthrust of the mountains that rose almost from the shore, and little more than a bow-shot away, the cave of the sea-nymphs, its entrance shielded by silvery-leaved olive trees. And with a heart that felt near to choking him, he flung himself down on his knees and kissed the sandy earth of home.

But soon his joy turned to anger, as Athene told him the sad state of the land that he had come back to, and the sorrows of Penelope, and how at present she had not even their young son to help her hold off her swarming suitors, for Telemachus was gone to seek news of his father from Menelaus and Helen of the Fair Cheeks.

"Sweet lady, tell me what I must do, for my wits fail me!" Odysseus cried, kneeling still, with his face bowed into his hands.

"First, let us hide all this treasure, before men see it and start to wonder as to its meaning," said Athene. So they carried all the gold cups and fine garments into the cave, and she closed the entrance with a stone.

Then she cast a spell of disguise upon Odysseus, so that his good clothes turned to rags, with a half-bald stag skin over all by way of a cloak, and she wrinkled his skin and made his eyes dull, so that he seemed again the beggar who had stolen into Troy to carry off its Luck.

"Now," she bade him, "go you across the island to the farm of Eumaeus your swineherd. He is old now, but still loyal to you. Bide there among the pigs, while I go to fetch home Telemachus."

And she was no longer there – only a quiver in the air behind her. And Odysseus turned his face toward the mountain tracks that led inland.

When he reached the farm, Eumaeus was sitting in his doorway making himself a new pair of oxhide brogues. His dogs ran out barking at the stranger with their hackles up and would have attacked him, but that their master ran up and drove them off with a shower of stones. He greeted the seeming beggarman kindly, and brought him into his own hut at the head of the farmyard, and gave him food and rough wine. And afterward, being glad of someone to talk to, he told him of the loss of the king, his master, and the haughtiness and greed of the young ruffians making themselves at home in the palace and trying to force themselves upon the queen in marriage. The swineherd had loved his master, and the story had become a deep grievance with him which, in the way of old men, he told over and over again to anyone with ears to listen.

Odysseus listened, as well he might, and when the story was over, he promised the old swineherd that his master was alive and would soon be returning home, for he had heard of him in his own wanderings.

Eumaeus did not believe him, for he thought that the beggar was only telling what he thought he would like to hear. But he listened courteously and later, when the herd-lads returned from the grazing land driving the pigs before them, and it was time for supper, he fed him a good meal of roast pork, as much of it as he could eat. And afterwards, Odysseus amused them all with tales of the Trojan war until it was time for sleep.

Meanwhile, Athene was in the palace of Menelaus, standing beside Telemachus as he lay wakeful in the night, troubled for his mother and wondering how things went at home. She told him that his mother had at last weakened and promised to marry one of the suitors, and that he must sail at once if he would keep her from doing so.

"Take a different sea-way home from the one that brought you here," she bade him, "for Antinous with a fast galley waits for you under the bluff of Same, eager to have your life. When you reach Ithaca, send your rowers on to the town. But you yourself must walk alone across the island to the farm of Eumaeus your swineherd, who is still loyal to you and your father."

So in the morning, Telemachus and his friend Pisistratus took their leave of Menelaus and Helen, who made them rich parting gifts of a golden cup and a silver mixing bowl. And Helen brought out a silken robe, the fairest of all that she herself had embroidered, and gave it into Telemachus' hands, saying, "A gift from me, dear boy, for your bride to wear when the day comes. Meanwhile, let it lie in your mother's care. All joy go with you – and Helen's love."

Just as they were on the edge of leaving, their chariot standing at the palace gates and the horses impatient and fidgeting under the yoke, an eagle came swooping from the mountain heights. He snatched up one of the white geese that were feeding on the grass nearby, swerved away with it low across the chariot horses, then upward and away.

"An omen, surely. But is it for you, my lord king, or for us two?" said Pisistratus, watching it grow small in the sky.

"For you, surely," said Helen of the Fair Cheeks. "Wait, and I will prophesy what the Great Ones put into my heart. As the eagle came down from the wild mountain heights and made an end of the fat farm-reared goose, so shall Odysseus return from his wilderness years and take vengeance on those who grow fat around his hearth."

Telemachus thanked her for her words of good omen and, mounting into the chariot beside Pisistratus, set out on the road home.

Next day they came to Pylos. Pisistratus drove straight to the harbour and set Telemachus down there with his guest-gifts, for he did not wish to come again to Nestor's palace, fearing that the good old man would seek to make him stay. He called up his rowers and went on board, and they set sail for Ithaca.

And when they made land-fall, he sent his crew on down the coast to the town, as the lady Athene had ordered, and himself walked up into the hills toward the swineherd's farm.

Odysseus and the swineherd had just roused up the fire to make the morning meal when a young man came in through the farm gate, and the dogs ran to meet him, yelping and fawning on him as he crossed the yard. The swineherd leapt up with a shout, oversetting the bowl in which he had been mixing wine and water, and ran to greet the newcomer. And looking after him Odysseus saw, just as Helen had seen it, the stranger's likeness to himself and to old Laertes. And he knew, his breath catching in his throat, that this was the son he had last seen as a babe in his mother's arms when the black ships sailed for Troy.

The swineherd was hugging Telemachus like a long-lost son, and Telemachus was thumping the old man on the back and demanding to know whether he was in time to stop his mother's marriage, both of them talking at the same time, as Eumaeus dragged him into the hut. Odysseus, mindful of his beggar's guise, would have clambered to his feet as the young man crossed the threshold, but the prince bade him sit down again, saying, "There's room enough in this place for two guests to sit beside the fire."

Eumaeus brought an armful of brushwood and spread a fleece over it for the latest comer. So they sat, all three of them, and made their morning meal on cold pig meat and wheaten bread, and wine in an ivy-wood bowl. And while they ate, the prince and the swineherd discussed what was to be done with the old beggar, who seemed to be so far gone into himself and so taken up with the food that he might as well have not been there at all.

In the end, they decided that Telemachus could not well take such a tattered creature to his mother's house, lest he should suffer insult and ill-usage from the rabble of young men there: and so Eumaeus should keep him at the farm, the prince sending up clothes and food that he might not be a burden there.

Then Telemachus bade the old swineherd go to the palace, and find means to tell his mother the queen that he was safely back from his journey.

He was scarcely gone on his errand when the dogs sprang up, whimpering, and crept with their tails down into the farthest corner of the hut, as bright-eyed Athene appeared in the doorway. Telemachus did not see her, only Odysseus and the dogs, who knew that some great presence was among them and were afraid.

Odysseus went out to the goddess, and she bade him tell his son who he was, now that they were alone together, and touched him with the golden rod she carried. Instantly he returned to his true seeming, and his rags became the kingly garments which it was fitting for him to wear, and he turned and went back into the hut.

Telemachus, looking up from beside the fire, saw the change in him and sprang up. "Stranger," he said in awe, "you are greatly altered from the old man who went out but a moment since. Surely you are one of the immortal gods!"

"No god," Odysseus told him, "but your father come home at last in beggar's guise to escape men's knowing, and now returned to his own form by the Lady of the Bright Eyes."

Telemachus shook his head. "You are not my father – you could not be!" And then, "I pray you, if you are not Odysseus, do not make our grief the more bitter by pretending."

"No pretending," his father said. "Believe this, and do not look for the coming of any other man, for I am Odysseus, and there is no other, nor ever has been!"

Then Telemachus let himself believe, and the two flung their arms about each other, weeping for joy.

In a while, sitting down again, Odysseus told his son as swiftly as might be of his wanderings and the gifts of the Phaeacians hidden in the sea-nymphs' cave; and with the story told, he asked for details of the suitors, what numbers they had to deal with and how they were armed, and the like.

One hundred and eight, Telemachus told him, and with them a faithless servant of his own, and the royal harper whom they had taken and forced to sing for their feasts. They were all strong young men who had brought their swords with them to their wooing, but no shields or body-armour.

"These are odds indeed!" said Odysseus. "But I do not doubt that we shall overcome them, for we have the Lady Athene for our friend, which is worth many men with swords."

So they fell to working out their plan of action.

Telemachus was to return next morning, and however badly the suitors behaved towards him, he must not allow himself to be drawn into any kind of open quarrel. And later in the day, Odysseus would come down in his beggar's guise and join the household, and when the right moment came he would give Telemachus a sign to take down the shields and helmets and fine weapons that hung on the walls of the great hall, and hide them away in a safe place.

"And what shall I say if that lordly rabble misses them?" his son asked.

"Say first that the smoke of the fire was spoiling them. And if they ask again, say that they are better out of the way, lest your mother's guests should grow quarrelsome in their wine."

And they laughed together.

"What else?" Telemachus asked.

Odysseus said, "Only remember to let no man or woman know that the old beggar in the corner is more than he seems!"

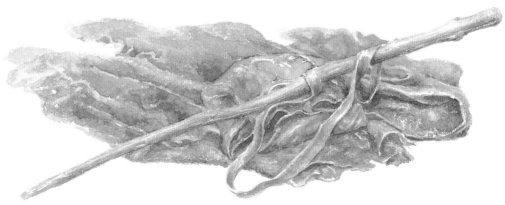

THE BEGGAR IN THE CORNER

Next morning, Telemachus went home. And there he found most of the suitors practising spear-throwing, while the rest were killing pigs for the morning meal.

They greeted him warmly enough; yet they saw that he was no longer the boy he had been, but a grown man and a danger to them. There was murder in their hearts, and he knew it, remembering the galley waiting under the bluffs of Same, though he gave no sign.

His mother, having been forewarned of his coming by Eumaeus, greeted him in her chamber, half-angry, half-weeping for joy that he was safely home. And Telemachus comforted her; told her of his journey and the news that he had gathered of his father and the promise that he would be home soon. He longed to tell her the whole truth, that he had been with Odysseus only that morning and had left him at the swineherd's farm, but he remembered his father's bidding and remained silent.

Meanwhile, Eumaeus had returned to the farm from his own errand at the palace; but Athene had again cast the beggarman's guise upon Odysseus, so that still the swineherd did not know his old master. The beggar was growing restless, eager to be going down to town and the royal house, for, said he, empty hills and grazing herds were of little use to him; he needed crowded places if he was to carry on his trade.

So, leaving the dogs and the herd-lads in charge of the farm, Eumaeus found his guest a staff to lean on, for the way was rough for old legs, and together they set off along the track that led down from the hills.

Coming near to the town, they met the royal goatherd, Melanthius, who supported the suitors, in the hope that whichever of them became king would be generous to his supporters. So when he met Eumaeus, who remained faithful to the old king and his son, he called him by evil names, scapegrace and wastrel, and tried to kick Odysseus off the path; and Odysseus was minded to kill him with his naked hands, but held back lest he betray himself. So they merely stepped round him and went peaceably on their way, leaving him to shout insults after them.

They had no other ill meeting with anyone and in a short while they came into the outer court of the palace.

Now, beside the doorway a pile of dung lay ready for carting to the fields, and on the warm pile an old dog lay outstretched and dozing: a great hound once, but now thin and full of vermin, his hunting days long behind him; and he raised his head and looked up as they paused close by. Man and hound looked at each other, and the old hound knew his master, even in beggar's guise, and flattened his ears and wagged his tail, though he had no strength to come towards him. And Odysseus knew his hound, Argus, who had been scarcely more than a pup when the black ships sailed.

Odysseus rubbed his eyes hastily with the back of his hand. "This is a sorry thing," he said to cover his grief, "to see a dog like this, lying in the dung-heap. He looks to have been a hunting dog in his day."

"He was that," said Eumaeus, "and in his day the young huntsmen used to take him out after deer and wild goats, even hares. But his master died in foreign parts, and the servants are heedless and take no care of him – especially in these evil times with the household in such disorder." And he went on into the house.

Odysseus stood a moment longer beside Argus, his dog. He would have squatted down and taken the old tired head on his knee, but there were many onlookers round about, and he could not. And in that instant a shudder ran through the gaunt body; Argus, having seen again the master he had waited for through nineteen years, was dead.

Odysseus walked on after Eumaeus. He did not enter the hall, his own hall, where the suitors were at supper and the harper playing, but sat down in the beggar's place on the high wooden threshold, his back against the door-pillar of polished cypress wood.

Telemachus saw him there, from his high seat beside the central hearth, and bade Eumaeus take him a wheaten loaf and a lump of pork. Odysseus ate the food, and then, thinking to test the suitors to see if there was any kindness among them, he took his filthy pouch and made his way up the hall, begging as he went. Some of the young lords tossed him crusts and bones; but one – it was Antinous, back from his empty watch below the bluffs of Same – caught up a stool and struck him on the shoulder with it.

"May death come upon Antinous before his wedding day!" said Odysseus. And there was an uneasy grumbling murmur from the rest, and spurts of laughter that was only half laughter and half something else. For they knew the dangers of ill-treating such a stray comer, who might well turn out to be a god in disguise.

Now, there were women slaves in the hall at the time; and so in a short while, word of what had happened reached Penelope in her chamber, and she was angry that such a thing should happen beneath her roof. Also, it had long been her custom to talk with every stranger and traveller who came that way, in the hope that they might have news of her lord. So she sent for Eumaeus and bade him bring the beggar to her chamber. But when Odysseus received the summons, he sent back word by the swineherd that he had been struck once in the hall and would not come into the house again until the rabble of suitors had gone home for the night. And to this the queen agreed, saying that she would meet him in the hall when the quiet time came.

Odysseus settled down in the doorway to wait. But he was not suffered to wait long in peace. For there was another beggar about the palace, who had been, as it were, the reigning beggar for a long time: a man named Irus, a big fellow, but with little muscle or mettle. Coming up and finding a newcomer on the threshold, he bade him be gone. "Off with you, before I drag you away by one foot!"

"There is room enough for both of us," said Odysseus peaceably.

But the other, red-faced with fury, shouted at him to get up and fight if he wanted to remain. And the suitors, who had finished eating and had turned to dancing and making merry in the court, thought that a fight between two beggars would be something to watch for a change. So they stamped and clapped for it to begin, promising that the winner should have his fill of the black puddings left from supper, and that he should be King Beggar and no one else should beg in his territory.

So Odysseus, seeing no help for it, stripped to the waist. And seeing the strength of his arms and shoulders, Irus began to have second thoughts, and would have called off the fight. But the suitors had formed a circle, shouting and laughing, and forced him on.

The fight was soon over. Irus swung a clumsy blow at Odysseus' shoulder, but Odysseus' fist took him cleanly below the left ear, and he fell, with blood trickling from his nose and mouth; and Odysseus dragged him aside from the doorway, and propped him carefully against the wall and left him there to bleed, while the suitors laughed and hailed the new King Beggar.

But when Odysseus, sickened by their horseplay, told them they would be wise to go home and stay there, lest the master of the house should return to find them making a pigsty of his hall, they turned ugly, and one of them, Eurymachus by name, flung a stool at him, which missed him as he ducked, and hit one of the cup-bearers instead, spilling the great mixing-bowl of wine, and all was uproar yet again.

At last the young men, sleepy with much food and drink, reeled away to their own sleeping places in the town. Then Odysseus and his son took down the fine weapons from the walls and carried them away to one of the storerooms below the house. And when they had been safely hidden away, Telemachus went off to sleep in his own chamber, which opened on to the inner courtyard.

But Odysseus sat on in the darkening hall where the fires were burning low, and waited for Penelope to come.

Her maidens came first, trooping in laughing and chattering among themselves to clear the remains of the feast. They were startled to find the old beggarman still sitting there, and one of them, Melantho, tried to shoo him out as though he had been something strayed in from the farmyard, threatening him with a shower of torches round his ears. But Penelope, entering close behind, heard this and scolded her, ordering the fire to be made up on the central hearth and a chair set for him beside it. And when he was seated, and the maidens had gone back to their own quarters, she sat down in her own chair spread with milky ram-skins, and began to question him as to who he was and where he came from.

Not being ready to tell her the truth, he told her another of his stories: how he was a Cretan prince who had not sailed with the black ships, and how Odysseus had been his guest on his way to Troy, while repairs were made to some of his fleet which had been damaged in a storm.

Penelope wept to hear even such ancient news. But many false stories had been told her by strangers in the years gone by. So, to test him, she said, "Tell me how my lord was dressed, for I long to hear all there is to hear about him."

Odysseus smiled within himself. But he answered her seriously enough. "He wore a double cloak of purple, held at the shoulder by a brooch with two sheathed pins to it, the brooch fashioned like a hunting dog holding down a struggling fawn. And beneath his cloak a silken tunic smooth as the inner skin of a peeled onion."

And Penelope wept afresh, for she had given that pin and the cloak and tunic to her lord at his setting out.

"Nay," said Odysseus, "no more tears, lady, for in these later wanderings that ill-fortune has brought upon me, I have heard again of Odysseus; how he still lives, he alone of all his company, and is on his way home to you even now."

Penelope dared not let herself believe, for she had believed too many times before. But she could not refuse the hope that he brought her, either; so in gratitude she called up Eurycleia, the old nurse, and bade her bring warm water and bathe the stranger's feet, which were dust-caked and chapped with long journeying.

Seeing who it was, when she brought the bowl, Odysseus drew back a little, and turned his face from the firelight.

"Foolish old woman that I am," Eurycleia mumbled softly through toothless gums, "I do this gladly, for the sake of my old master, who may have sorely needed some woman to do the same for him in a foreign land. Indeed, clean and freshly clad, it is in my mind that you might look much as he used to do. Aye, you have the look – even your hands and feet —"

"Others who have seen us both have said much the same thing," Odysseus said quickly.

But in the same instant she broke off her mumbling, looking down as she pushed his rags aside, at the long white scar which began just above his knee and ran up and out towards his hip: the scar of a boar's tusk, gained on the hunting trail when he was little more than a boy. Eurycleia recognised the old wound immediately.

"Oh my child!" she whispered. "Oh my master!" She was the second, as Argus had been the first, to know him again in his beggar's guise.

She let his foot fall back with a splash into the water, and was already turning, her mouth open to cry out the glad news to Penelope, sitting close by; but Athene had drawn the queen's thoughts away from what was happening beside the hearth, for it was not yet time for her to know the truth. And Odysseus set his hand on the old woman's throat, while with the other he drew her closer. "Silence, old nurse, would you be the death of me?"

And looking at him, she understood, and nodded. "Silent as a stone, my dearie." And with shaking hands she went on with her task.

When she had bathed his feet and rubbed them with oil, and had gone her way bearing the basin with her, Penelope turned to the stranger again and began to tell him her sorrows, and how, if Odysseus did not soon return, she must yield at last and take one of the suitors for her new lord. But how should she choose among them when in truth she wanted none?

"Call a contest of some kind," Odysseus said harshly, "and give yourself to the winner."

She made no reply for a while, paying great attention to her spinning. But in a while she let the spindle fall idle, and looked up. "My lord's own bow is still in the house," she said. "A great bow that few men but he can draw. In his young days, I recall, he would sometimes take twelve of the axe-rings that men use for target practice and games of bowmanship, set them up in a row and shoot an arrow straight through all twelve, for a show of skill. So I will make my contest, and whichever man can best string my lord's bow and loose his shafts through the ranged axe-rings, that man I will take for my new lord, and him I will go with, bidding farewell to this house that has been my home since I came to it as a bride."

"Then hold the contest tomorrow," Odysseus said. "Even so, it is in my mind that Odysseus himself may well be here before a lesser man can draw his bow."

Penelope gave him a long look, then rose and left the hall, climbing to her own chamber where her bower-women awaited her.

THE ARCHERY CONTEST

ODYSSEUS PASSED THE rest of the night on piled sheepskins in the portico, where he lay wakeful, his head racing with plans for overcoming his enemies, until the Lady Athene brought him the sleep he sorely needed.

In the morning he rose early, and prayed to Zeus the All-Father for a sign of his favour. Scarce was his prayer finished than Zeus sent him a peal of thunder out of a clear sky. Then he heard the voice of a woman grinding corn close by, that the suitors might have their fill of fresh bread; grinding still though all her fellows had finished, because she was old and weak and had not yet filled her allotted number of baskets. "Lord Zeus," she said, "surely that thunder was a sign of your favour to some lucky man. Let me share in his good fortune. Grant that this be the last time I grind for the young lords who make merry in my master's hall, and who have worn me out with grinding for them! May this be their last feast!"

And at the thunderclap and the woman's words, Odysseus' heart lifted and grew strong within him.

Soon the servants had started work, sweeping and sprinkling the earthen floors and spreading purple coverings on the chairs, sponging down the tables and cleaning the wine-cups under the watchful eye of Eurynome the housekeeper, while others went to fetch water from the well.

Then Eumaeus appeared with pigs from the farm, and hailed Odysseus like an old friend; while they chatted together, Melanthius the goatherd

arrived with beasts for slaughter, and greeted Odysseus in his own insolent fashion. "What, still here? Best take yourself off, before I have to help you on your way!"

Then came Philoetius the cowherd with cattle for the table, who, hearing what ill-treatment the strange beggar had had from the suitors, marched straight up to him and caught his hand, saying, "Here's a welcome to you, old fellow. You have come on hard times, but luck changes; you may go up any day, just as these lordlings who guzzle my best cattle may go down."

Lastly came the suitors themselves, like a noisy gaggle of geese, crowding in to the morning meal, and Telemachus with a couple of his favourite hounds at heel and a hunting-spear in his hand, who bade Odysseus take his seat just within the hall and ordered the servants to give him a fair share of the food.

Ctesippus, one of the suitors, said, "His fair share he has had already, but I will give him something extra," and threw an ox-foot at Odysseus with all his might. But the beggar only leaned aside, and the ox-foot struck the wall where he had been.

Telemachus protested furiously at this, though he was only one against their many, and he did not forget his orders to keep the peace until the right moment came. Yet at his protest, a strange mood swept through the crowded hall like a great wind rising, and the suitors began to laugh

95

and weep wildly both at the same time, without knowing why. But the Lady Athene who had sent that mood upon them, she knew why.

And a man of the household, who at times had the second sight, cried out upon them, "Unhappy men! I see darkness all about you, and tears are on your cheeks, and all the air full of the sound of mourning; the walls and floors are splashed with blood, and in the forecourt your ghosts are hurrying down to the Underworld, and the sun is blotted from the skies."

But they only laughed more wildly, and bade him go out into the town if he found it so dark in the palace.

"That I will do," said the seer, "for death is coming fast to every one of you, and I want no more of your company!" And he got up and strode out of the hall.

The suitors nudged each other and exchanged glances, still rocking with laughter, and began to jeer at Telemachus, baiting him in every way they could think of. But Telemachus kept his mouth shut and his eyes on his father, waiting for the signal that the time was come.

Then into the hall came Penelope, bearing her lord's great horn bow and a quiver well stocked with arrows, followed by her women carrying her chest with the twelve axes. She took her stand by one of the great pillars that upheld the roof, and scornfully issued her challenge.

"Lordlings, since it seems that I must wed with one of you, it is my pleasure to hold a contest to decide which one. Therefore, whichever of you can best string this bow, which belonged to my true marriage-lord, and send an arrow straight through the rings of these twelve axes as they stand ranged in order, to that man I will give myself."

Telemachus sprang up before all the rest, claiming the right to loose the first arrow. "And if I succeed, not one of you shall take the queen my mother from her own house!"

But first the targets must be set up. The prince flung off his cloak, then called for a spade, and dug a long narrow trench in the earthen floor, taking care that it should run exactly toward the place where his father sat just within the doorway. He planted the twelve axes along it, checking that their line was true, each ring exactly behind its neighbour, and stamped the earth round them.

Then, picking up the bow and quiver, he took his stand on the high threshold. Three times he tried to string the great bow, and three times he failed. A fourth time he tried, with clenched teeth and the strength of desperation; and that time he seemed like to succeed; but the old beggar made him a small quick sign with one hand, and he laid the weapon down, shaking his head. "Alas! I have not my father's strength."

Then one after another they all tried, each man rising in his turn and taking his stand before the threshold. And one after another they failed. After maybe the tenth or twelfth failure, Antinous called for more wood on the fire and a pot of grease to warm the bow and make it supple, for surely it had grown dry and rigid with lack of use. And they warmed and greased the horns of the bow and tried again, but with no better luck than before.

While this was going on, Eumaeus and the cowherd, getting bored with watching something that was getting nowhere, went out past the squatting beggar into the courtyard. Odysseus rose and went quietly after them; and outside in the portico he spoke to them, low-voiced: "If the Lord Odysseus were to return and need your aid, would you fight for him, or for that rabble in there?"

"For the Lord Odysseus!" they said, both in the same breath. "The gods grant that he come – and before it is too late!"

Then Odysseus pulled up his ragged tunic, and showed them his thigh. "Do you recognise that scar?"

They stared and snatched at their breath; then, weeping joyful tears, they flung themselves upon him and embraced him like a brother.

But after a few moments Odysseus dropped his arms and bade them stand back, lest anyone should pass and see their joyful reunion and think it odd. "Now," said he, "I am going back into the hall. Follow me, Eumaeus, and when I ask leave to try my own strength and skill, do you bring the bow and set it in my hands, no matter who may say you nay. And Philoetius, go you and make fast the door that leads from the forecourt out on to the road. And when it is done, do you also come to join me."

And he went back into the crowded and noisy hall, where the suitors were still trying to string the great bow. Even as he came again to his place within the doorway, Antinous was suggesting that they should put the contest off until the next day, and sacrifice to Apollo the Far-Shooter before they tried again. But the beggar in the doorway spoke up and asked to be allowed to try his strength and skill. The young lords laughed uproariously at the mere idea, and told him too much good food and wine had gone to his head, and threatened to send him off in a ship to King Echetus, who liked to feast on human flesh, since there seemed no other way of getting rid of him.

But Penelope, still standing beside the central column, raised her voice, calm and cool, saying that the beggar was a guest in her house even as they were, and must try with the rest of them if he wished.

"And will you wed him if he succeeds?" someone shouted, amid more laughter.

"I do not think he would expect that," said Penelope. "But I will give him a warm new cloak and a sword and spear, and aid him on his way to wherever he wishes to go."

Then Telemachus said that he would give the beggar a prize – even the bow itself if he wished, for it was his to give. And when his mother the queen protested at this, he bade her go to her own quarters and work at her weaving among her maidens, for that was woman's work, and to leave the matter of weapons to the men.

Penelope was startled, never before having heard him speak in that way, like the master of the house; and she went upstairs quietly, her maidens about her, to her own chambers in the women's part of the palace.

In the hall, Eumaeus was carrying the bow to Odysseus, but the suitors made such a threatening clamour that he paused halfway and would have laid it down, fearing for his life. But Telemachus shouted to him above the hubbub, "Get on with that bow, old fellow. You cannot obey all of us, and since I am your master it had better be me!"

And Eumaeus gathered his courage and walked on down the hall, and laid the great bow together with its quiver in Odysseus' hands. Then, on a private word from his old master, he went and bade Eurycleia lock the door of the women's quarters, and when he had seen it done, returned to the hall. Meanwhile Philoetius had made fast the courtyard gates, securing them with a ship's rope that was lying in the colonnade. Then he too returned to the hall, and rejoined the swineherd close to Odysseus, who, heedless of the suitors' mockery and insults, was turning the bow this way and that, making sure that it was in good condition, and that the ibex horns of which it was made were free from worm.

When he was satisfied, he set the butt under his instep, and bent the bow and strung it as easily as a minstrel restringing his lyre. A murmur of angry dismay rose from the crowded hall. He tried the string, hearing the twang of it like the call-note of a swallow. He took up the arrow that he had already drawn from the quiver beside him, and nocked it to the string, and, not rising from the stool on which he sat, raised the bow

and drew and loosed all in one swift movement. And the arrow sped on its way, passing cleanly through all twelve axe-rings.

"Your beggarly guest has done no dishonour to your father's bow," he said to Telemachus. "But now, if we wish to feast again in the king's hall, it is time that we hunted and made the kill." And so saying, he got up from the stool, giving his shoulders a little shake, like a man getting ready for action.

And Telemachus came up the hall to stand beside him, his hunting spear ready in his hand.

THE SLAYING OF THE SUITORS

ODYSSEUS TOOK ONE LEAP, and was standing on the broad high threshold. He tipped the arrows from the quiver out at his feet and, shouting in triumph, "Now I shoot at another mark, that no archer has yet found!" he aimed and loosed another shaft. Antinous still held the golden cup that he had been drinking from, and it fell with a clatter as he sprawled backward, the arrow in his throat.

The suitors leapt to their feet, shouting threats and staring wildly about them for the shields and spears that should have been hanging on the walls. But the walls were bare.

And already Odysseus had another arrow nocked to his bowstring. "Dogs!" he shouted. "You thought that I should not return from Troy, and so you wasted my goods and tried to force yourselves upon my wife! All things seemed to go your way and you had no decent fear of the gods, but now the time of reckoning, the death-time, has come upon you all!"

"Draw your swords and use the tables for shields!" Eurymachus shouted to his fellows. "After me, and we'll drive him from the doorway!" And drawing his sword, he rushed upon Odysseus with a yell.

But Odysseus let fly the arrow from his bow, and even as the man leapt forward the bronze barb was in his heart, and he crashed down among overturned stools and spilled wine. Amphinomus came next, but Telemachus' flung spear brought him to the ground, his arms and legs flailing for a few moments before he lay still.

102

Telemachus shouted to his father that he was away to bring weapons from the store-room; and Odysseus, nocking another arrow to his bowstring, nodded without turning his gaze from the baying crowd. "Go quickly, while I have arrows left to hold them from the doorway."

And Telemachus ran and returned with all speed, clanging with shields and spears and helmets for the two of them and for Eumaeus and Philectius.

They armed themselves under cover of Odysseus' arrow-fire; and when his arrows were gone, Odysseus took up his own armour while the other three gave him the like cover with their spears.

But Melanthius the goatherd knew a way of reaching the store-rooms secretly, and, seeing no hope for his own life if the suitors were slain or overcome, he slipped away, and returned laden like a pack-mule with armour and spears for them.

Odysseus, seeing armed men beginning to appear among the mob, called to Eumaeus and the cowherd to run to the armour store and find out who was helping their enemies. The two men ran; and in the armoury they found Melanthius collecting yet more weapons to carry out to the suitors. They bound him with bale-ropes and, throwing the end of the last rope over a rafter, hauled him up and left him swinging until they should know what was their lord's will concerning him. Then they made all haste back to take their places with Odysseus and his son: four men holding the doorway against the furious mob of suitors in the hall.

Now the goddess Athene once more took a hand, appearing in the guise of a boyhood friend of the king's, to cry him on as a charioteer cries on his team at the races, before she changed shape into a swallow and fluttered up to perch on the main tie-beam of the roof. From there, watching all that went on, she sent out her power so that when the suitors, led now by Agelaus, the strongest among them, began to throw their spears in volleys, six at a time, they missed their mark, while the spears thrown by the four in the doorway killed each its man.

Again the suitors threw their spears, and this time Telemachus took a flesh wound, little more than a scratch, while another spear, flying above Eumaeus' shield, just nicked his shoulder in passing.

But Odysseus and his three in the doorway, sending one more flight into the thick of the mob, brought down each one the man he aimed at.

Then, their spears spent, they drew their swords, and led by Odysseus charged up the hall into the midst of their enemies, killing as they went.

At that same instant, high in the crown of the roof above him, Pallas Athene changed shape again, to appear in all her fearful splendour, holding up the deadly aegis that strikes terror into the hearts of all beholders.

Horror and awe laid hold of the suitors, and instead of standing to receive Odysseus' charge, they scattered through the hall like a herd of cattle stampeded by gadflies. And the four champions leapt upon them and harried them to and fro, slaying all about them.

Medon the herald, who had tried to serve the royal house even while he tried not to fall out with the suitors, crept from under a table where he had been hiding muffled in a freshly-flayed oxhide, and flung himself at Telemachus' feet, begging for mercy. And Phemius the minstrel came with his lyre and clung to Odysseus' knees, crying, "I only sang for them because they forced me – the prince your son will tell you so. Let me sing for you as I have so often longed to do!"

And Odysseus spared them both, and sent them out into the courtyard, where they crouched together before the household altar.

The king turned back to whatever more of the battle waited for him. But the fighting was over, and the suitors to the very last one lay dead, piled in heaps up and down the hall like fish on a seashore where they have been netted and drawn to land.

Then Telemachus went and fetched the old nurse Eurycleia, who, when she saw Odysseus standing bloodied like a slaughterman, and around him all the piled dead, raised a great screeching of triumph and delight. But Odysseus checked her, saying, "It is an ill thing to gloat aloud over dead men. Rejoice if you will, but silently."

Then he bade Telemachus and the servants carry the dead into the courtyard, and he set the women slaves under the eye of Eurynome the housekeeper to clean up the hall, swabbing the blood and filth from the floor and washing down the walls and seats and tables.

And the men took Melanthius and slew him in the courtyard, after which they washed themselves, and Odysseus called for sulphur to be burned on the fires to fumigate the house. The door of the women's quarters being now unlocked, Penelope's own bower-women came out into the hall with torches in their hands, for it was dark by this time. They knew their old master, and wept for joy to see him standing again in his own place, and kissed his hands and forehead. And he knew them, every one, for they were not young maidens, but had been with Penelope before ever he sailed for Troy.

But Penelope herself did not come, for she was still in the deep sleep that grey-eyed Athene had cast upon her before the fighting in the hall began. And the old nurse, unable to wait a moment longer, ran to tell her all that there was to tell, tripping and stumbling on the stair, and laughing for joy as she ran.

"Come and see the thing that you have longed for so long: Odysseus back in his own hall and all your suitors lying slain!"

Penelope roused and sat up.

"Old nurse," she said, "you must be addled in your wits to bring me such a tale as that! And you have woken me from the sweetest sleep that I have known since my lord sailed for Troy!"

"No tale but the truth, mistress dear!" protested the old woman. "The Lord Odysseus is in his hall! He is that beggar whom your suitors so insulted – oh, but Telemachus knew his father, he can tell you —"

Then Penelope sprang from her bed and kissed her, but even as she did so, she felt the news too shining and wonderful to be true, and she dared not let herself believe it. "What proof have either of you that it is in truth my lord himself, and not some god who has taken on his likeness to take revenge upon my suitors for their evil-doing? Or indeed some wicked man trading upon his likeness to Odysseus while my own dear marriage-lord lies dead far away?"

"If so, god or man has learned to imitate the hunting scar on his thigh so well that my hands knew it again even before my eyes saw it!" shrilled the old woman.

But still Penelope dared not quite believe. She drew her breath long and shaking, and said, "Then let us go down and see my son, and the suitors lying slain. And the man who slew them."

And with Eurycleia following, she went down the stairway and into the great hall, where Odysseus, still in his rags and foul with battle-blood, stood leaning against one of the tall roof-columns beside the fire. She seated herself at the other side of the hearth, and looked at him in the firelight. But still, even meeting his eyes, she could not be sure of him, and she was afraid. And as yet no word passed between them.

To give her time, Odysseus turned to the next thing, and bade her women fetch the minstrel. And when he came fearfully in from the courtyard, Odysseus bade the man make music for dancing in the hall, that any of the townsfolk passing by might think that a wedding-feast was going on. For by the law of the blood feud, the kinsmen of the slain suitors must come to avenge them when they heard of their deaths; and in this way he might at least gain a night's breathing space.

And when the dancing had begun, he allowed Eurynome to wash and anoint him and bring him fresh garments so that he looked like himself again. And he sat down in his own high seat beside the fire; and again he looked across at Penelope.

Yet even now, Penelope dared not be sure, but sat still as a figure of painted wood, looking back at him as though he were a stranger.

Then Odysseus said, "Surely you are the fairest but most cruel queen in all the world, to harden your heart against me when I come home at last after all these weary years!" And to Eurycleia he cried out harshly, "Old nurse, I am weary. Make me up a bed in some corner, for I must sleep, and it seems that this night I must sleep alone."

At that, Penelope knew suddenly how she could test him once and for all. If he knew the thing that only he and she and the oldest and most trusted of their servants could possibly know, then she would have no doubts left. "Do as he bids, old nurse," she said, "make up a bed outside the bridal chamber. Bring the bed out of that chamber for him."

Odysseus knew what she was about, and smiled in his heart. But he pretended to be angry. "How can anyone bring our marriage-bed from the place where it stands? Did I not build it myself, with a rooted and growing olive tree for one of the corner posts? Only by cutting down the tree could that bedstead be moved!"

As he spoke, Penelope's last doubts fled away and she left her chair on the far side of the fire, and came and flung her white arms round Odysseus' neck, and clung to him as though she could never let go, kissing him and begging, "Do not be angry with me! I have feared so much during all these years that some man might come, looking like you, and trick my heart into believing what I so longed to believe!"

And holding her close in the great chair beside the hearth, Odysseus told her of his wanderings, and his longing to come home to her, which had been with him in so many strange places. And lastly, lest hearing it at a later time she should be grieved, he told her how the soul of Tiresias had foretold to him, in the realm of Hades, that one day, before he finally came to rest in his own home, he must take an oar over his shoulder, and set out again on his voyaging: a land voyage this time, wandering through strange lands from city to city until he met some man who had never seen the sea or a ship and mistook the oar for a winnowing fan. "Then I must plant my oar in the earth," he said, "and sacrifice a ram and a bull and a breeding boar to Poseidon, and so I shall be free of the sea-god's wrath at last."

"If the gods will protect you and bring you home safe again in the end, then there is no more cause for grieving," said Penelope.

And the great bed with its olive-tree corner post being spread with fresh coverings and ready for them by then, they went to their own chamber, leaving the dancers in the hall behind them as though it really were a marriage-feast. And Eurynome, with lighted torches in her hands, went before them to lead the way.

PEACE IN THE ISLANDS

IN THE MORNING Odysseus woke early, knowing he had things that must still be attended to. He bade Penelope gather all the women into her own chambers and bide there quietly, letting no one in, until his return. He set all the men of the household on guard; and with Telemachus and the swineherd and cowman, all of them fully armed, he set off for the family farm among the hills where his father now lived.

When they came near to the clustered farm buildings, Odysseus told the other three to go up to the house and warn the housekeeper to make a meal ready. Then he made his way down through the steep orchard to the terraced vineyard where he was sure his father would be. The old man was there sure enough, in a weather-worn tunic, and leggings of much-patched leather to guard his shins from brambles, hard at work digging round the roots of his vines. He was quite alone, for his servants had gone to gather loose stones to build up the terrace wall; and he did not look up until Odysseus checked close beside him.

"Hard at work, old man? I can see there's not much you don't know about growing things," said Odysseus. "Never have I seen vines in better shape than these. Tell me now, whose slave are you, and who is the master of this place?" (For yet again he needed to know how people might think of his return, before he told them who he was.)

Laertes was astonished to see a man in war-gear in that peaceful vineyard; but he gathered himself together and answered, "No man's slave,

but the lord of this farm and its gardens, as once I was lord of all Ithaca
and the islands; for I am Laertes, the father of the great Odysseus, who
has been too long away, unheard of and unseen. But one question
answered deserves another; so tell me, stranger, who you are and from
what country you are come."

"I am from Sicily," Odysseus told him, "and there I met with your son
on his voyage back from Troy. He was my guest for a while, but that
was five years ago, and I had hoped to find him here, returned to his own
land long since."

The old man stooped down among his vines and wept, casting the fine
dark earth over his grey head. "If he has not returned to us from Sicily
in five long years, assuredly he must be dead."

Then Odysseus' heart melted, and he lifted and caught his father to
him, saying, "Father, do you not know me after nineteen years?"

But even looking into his face, Laertes found it hard to believe, just as
Penelope had done. "If you are indeed my son," he said at last, "give me
some proof, that I may be sure."

And Odysseus pulled back the fold of his kilt and showed the silvery
scar that the boar's tusk had left on his thigh. Then, looking round the
gardens, he said, "Come, and I will show you the trees you gave me for
my own, one summer afternoon when they were saplings and I was a little
boy running with the dogs at your heels. Mine are the thirteen pear trees

over there, and those ten apple trees, and forty of those figs. And you promised me that one day I should have these fifty rows of vines."

Then Laertes' old knees trembled under him and his heart almost burst for joy, so that he would have fallen, if Odysseus had not caught him and held him fast.

But when his head cleared, the first words he spoke were a warning: "There is wild work waiting for you when you come to your own house!"

"I have been there already, and the work is done," said Odysseus. "My father, the suitors are slain who have wasted my goods and persecuted my wife for so long."

But despite his joy at hearing it, the news brought another trouble into the old man's mind. "Then, few as we are, how shall we meet their kinsmen when they come upon us seeking vengeance?"

"Enough to worry about that when the time comes," said Odysseus. "Meanwhile, let us go back to the house, where I sent Telemachus ahead to see that food is made ready for us."

So back to the house they went, and there they found Telemachus and the other two already carving meat hot from the fire, and mixing the wine. And Laertes washed and put on fresh garments brought out for him by the housekeeper.

"I hope I may be as strong and as good to look upon when I am your age," Odysseus said, as they sat down to eat.

"Would that I were as strong as I was at your age, and could have stood beside you in yesterday's fight!" returned the old man.

Scarcely had they begun to eat when Dolius, the housekeeper's husband, and their three sons returned hungry from their stone-gathering. And when their first astonishment at their lord's return was over, Odysseus and Dolius greeted each other like the old friends they were, and the sons came with gladness to take his hands; and they settled down joyfully together to their noontide meal.

By now, word of Odysseus' return and what had happened in the palace was out and had run from end to end of the town and the island too, and the mourning kinsfolk of the slain suitors gathered at Odysseus' gate.

They bore away their own dead for burial, while the bodies of those who had come from the other islands were loaded into boats and sent back to their own homes.

Then the kinsfolk met together in the town's assembly-place, and as soon as they were gathered, Eupeithes, the father of Antinous the first-fallen of all the suitors, stood up in their midst and denounced Odysseus as their enemy. For he had returned without the companions who had sailed with him and without the ships; and now he had slaughtered the pick of their young men. Sorrow he had brought upon Ithaca. "Our honour will be gone, and our names will stink in the nostrils of those who come after us, if we do not follow him now and avenge our sons and brothers!"

One old man of more wisdom than the rest cried out against them that the young men had deserved their fate; but the others ran for their weapons; and, forming up behind Eupeithes, they set out for the royal farm, where they knew that Odysseus had gone earlier that morning.

Meanwhile, in the farmhouse, they had just finished their meal when one of Dolius' sons, who was standing in the doorway, called back over his shoulder that he saw spears in the sunlight, coming up the track.

Then all the rest sprang up, Odysseus and Telemachus, the faithful swineherd and cowman, the farmhands, and with them the two old men, Dolius and Laertes, a band of twelve in all. They caught up the weapons that were kept ready, and, being minded to fight in the open rather than seek to defend the farm, they opened the gates and, with Odysseus leading, sallied out to meet the enemy.

At that moment, Athene gave them her help one more time.

First she breathed daring into Laertes, telling him, "Laertes, dearest friend, pray to the Lord Zeus, and to the Lady of the Bright Eyes, then swiftly let fly your spear!"

And Laertes, who had not handled a weapon in battle for many a long year, felt the strength and skill flow back into him. He sent up a swift prayer, and as the advancing warriors came within throwing distance, drew back his spear and hurled it at Eupeithes. The bronze point passed through the cheek-guard of his helmet and into his head, and he crashed to the ground, his armour clanging upon him as he fell.

The men who followed him hesitated an instant, checked by his fall, and Odysseus and Telemachus together sprang upon their front rank, swords in hand and with their great spears at the ready. But Athene cried out in their midst, halting both bands of warriors, "Men of Ithaca, break off this fighting and fall back from each other, before more blood is spilled!"

At the voice of the goddess, panic struck through the men who had come for vengeance. They flung down their weapons and turned to run; but Odysseus had the smell of battle in his nostrils, and he raised his terrible war-cry and leapt after them like a hound on his quarry. But Zeus let fly a flaming bolt that struck the ground before his feet. And Athene cried out to him to stop, lest he anger Zeus the Lord of Thunder, the father of all the gods.

Then Odysseus' head cooled, and he obeyed her with a glad heart, and his son and his father and the warriors behind him. They sheathed their swords and stood leaning on their spear-shafts, and the men who had come to avenge their sons and brothers checked in their flight and turned back.

So Pallas Athene of the Shining Eyes made peace between them with all the proper rites and sacrifices; peace in Ithaca and among the islands.

LAND OF THE DEAD

ITALY

Monte Circeo ▲
CIRCE, THE ENCHANTRESS

▲ Mt Vesuvius
THE SIRENS

Aeolian Islands
AEOLUS, LORD OF THE WINDS

Straits of Messina
**SCYLLA &
CHARYBDIS**

Sicily
HYPERION, THE SUN LORD

▲
Mt Etna
THE CYCLOPES

Gozo
CALYPSO

Jerba
THE LOTUS-EATERS

LIBYA

RIVER OCEANUS

HOW TO PRONOUNCE THE GREEK NAMES

The letter *e* is pronounced long, as in "me", but when marked ĕ it is pronounced short, as in "wet".

The letters *i* and *y* are pronounced *ea* as in "bead", or *i* as in "bin".

The letters *eu* together are pronounced like the word "you".

The letters *au* together are pronounced *ow* as in "how".

The letters *ae, oe* together are pronounced like the *e* in "me".

The letters *ei* together are pronounced like the word "eye".

The letters *ch* are pronounced like *c*, as in "chord".

The letter *g* is pronounced like a *j*, as in "giant".

The letters *rh* are pronounced like *r*, as in "rat".

The accent is on the syllable marked ´.

These are some of the more difficult pronunciations:

Achílles

Agamĕmnon

Agĕlá-us

Alcíno-us

Amphínomus

Antíno-us

Aphrodíte

Áres

Āréte (Ah-reé-tee)

Athéne

Charýbdis

Círce

Ctesíppus

Ĕchĕtus

Eumaé-us

Eupeíthes

Euryceí-a

Eurýlochus

Eurýmachus

Eurýnome

Íno

Írus

Íthaca

La-értes

La-ódamas

Mĕnĕlá-us

Odýsseus

Nausicá-a (Nowsicáy-a)

Phae-ácia (Phee-áysha)

Pháros

Phémius

Phoenícia (Pheenísha)

Pisístratus

Poseídon

Pýlos

Scýlla (Silla)

Sísyphus

Tirĕsias

Rosemary Sutcliff